Golf
Annika's
Way

Golf
Annika's Way

by ANNIKA SORENSTAM

with the editors of
GOLF MAGAZINE

To John,

Need a new partner? Call me.

[signature]

GOTHAM BOOKS

G O T H A M   B O O K S

Published by Penguin Group (USA) Inc.
375 Hudson Street, New York, New York 10014, U.S.A.
Penguin Group (Canada), 10 Alcorn Avenue, Toronto, Ontario, Canada M4V 3B2
(a division of Pearson Penguin Canada Inc.); Penguin Books Ltd, 80 Strand, London WC2R 0RL, England;
Penguin Ireland, 25 St Stephen's Green, Dublin 2, Ireland (a division of Penguin Books Ltd);
Penguin Group (Australia), 250 Camberwell Road, Camberwell, Victoria 3124, Australia (a division of
Pearson Australia Group Pty Ltd); Penguin Books India Pvt Ltd, 11 Community Centre, Panchsheel Park,
New Delhi—110 017, India; Penguin Group (NZ), Cnr Airborne and Rosedale Roads, Albany,
Auckland, New Zealand (a division of Pearson New Zealand Ltd); Penguin Books (South Africa)
(Pty) Ltd, 24 Sturdee Avenue, Rosebank, Johannesburg 2196, South Africa.
Penguin Books Ltd, Registered Offices: 80 Strand, London WC2R 0RL, England

• • •

Published by Gotham Books, a division of Penguin Group (USA) Inc.
First printing, October 2004
1   3   5   7   9   10   8   6   4   2
Copyright © Esch & Stam, Inc., 2004
All rights reserved

• • •

PHOTO CREDITS
All photography by Fred Vuich unless otherwise noted.
AP/Wide World Photos pp. 20, 46–47, 212–213, 132–133, 170, 233;
Matt Rourke/Getty Images pp. 16–17; Sven Nackstrand/Getty Images p. 204; Scott Halleran/Getty Images pp. 216–217, 230–231;
David Cannon/Getty Images pp. 222–223; Warren Little/Getty Images p. 272; Doug Pensinger/Getty Images p. 272 (inset);
Other contributing photographers: Courtesy of Sorenstam family pp. 2, 4, 5, 6, 7, 8, 9, 10, 11, 12, 13, 15, 18;
Sam Greenwood pp. VI (3), 61, 108, 111, 112, 113, 115, 118, 120 (2), 121 (2), 127, 218, 221, 242, 256 (2), 258, 259, 265;
Mark Ashman pp. 244–245 (3), 248, 249, 250, 251, 252, 253, 254, 255, 257 (2), 260, 261, 264, 266, 267, 269;
Keiichi Sato pp. 178, 215

• • •

Gotham Books and the skyscraper logo are trademarks of Penguin Group (USA) Inc.
VISION54™ is a registered trademark of VISION54 Coaching for the Future, Inc.

• • •

LIBRARY OF CONGRESS CATALOGING-IN-PUBLICATION DATA
Sorenstam, Annika, 1970–
Golf Annika's way / by Annika Sorenstam with the editors of GOLF MAGAZINE.
p. cm.
Includes index.
ISBN 1-59240-076-0 (hardcover : alk. paper)
1. Golf. 2. Sorenstam, Annika, 1970– I. GOLF MAGAZINE (New York, N.Y. : 1991) II. Title.
GV965.S6724 2004
796.352'3--dc22   2004006969
Printed in the United States of America

• • •

Set in Hiroshige
Designed by Judy Turziano

• • •

ACKNOWLEDGMENTS
My thanks go to Gotham Books and to *GOLF MAGAZINE* for their efforts in bringing this book to print.
In particular, my gratitude goes to William M. Shinker, Senior Vice President and Publisher, and to Brendan Cahill, Editor, of Gotham Books.
As for my collaborators at *GOLF MAGAZINE*, I especially want to recognize and thank Senior Editor Tara Gravel and Associate Editor Dave Allen
for their help with the writing, and Photographers Fred Vuich, Sam Greenwood, and Mark Ashman, as well as Kevin Cook, Editor,
and Julie Hansen, Vice President, *GOLFONLINE* Business Development. I also appreciate the writing assistance of Marino Parascenzo.
I also want to thank my coach, Henri Reis, and my trainer, Kai Fusser (kaifusser.com), for their valuable assistance with this book, and I am grateful to
Lake Nona Golf & Country Club and General Manager Eric Allain for the use of their facilities for the photography.

• • •

This book is printed on acid-free paper. ∞

With love to those who mean the most to me,

my father and mother, Tom and Gunilla,

my sister, Lotta, and especially to

my husband, David.

Contents

FOREWORD • VIII, XI / PROLOGUE • XII

⊰⊱ AT THE TEE ⊰⊱

1 My Journey
GOLF—IT'S CHILD'S PLAY • 3

2 Back to Basics
FUNDAMENTALS FOR EVERY SWING • 23

⊰⊱ THE FULL SWING ⊰⊱

3 Driving
HIT IT LONGER AND STRAIGHTER • 45

4 Accurate Irons
HOW TO HIT MORE GREENS • 73

5 Fairway Woods
A LOFTY ALTERNATIVE • 91

6 Wedge Play
HOW TO KNOCK IT STIFF • 109

✦◁══ THE SHORT GAME ══▷✦

Turn 3 into 2

CHIP AND PITCH IT CLOSE • *131*

Bunker Play

HOW TO GET OUT OF THE SAND • *159*

Putting

NEVER THREE-PUTT AGAIN • *179*

✦◁══ THE MENTAL SIDE ══▷✦

On the Course

A BEAUTIFUL MIND GAME • *205*

Vision54™

WHY NOT BIRDIE EVERY HOLE? • *231*

✦◁══ STAYING IN SHAPE ══▷✦

Getting Fit

WORKOUT TIPS TO HELP YOUR GAME • *247*

Foreword

I n 1999, Annika Sorenstam and I were attending a corporate outing in San Francisco when she asked me if I would look at her putting. I gave her a couple of ideas to start off with, and then we got together a couple of weeks later at Bighorn Golf Club in Palm Springs for a serious session.

When I teach someone to putt, I use the words "feel" and "roll" instead of words like "try" and "hit." Annika tended to putt mechanically, and I wanted her to reach into her subconscious and feel the ball roll so that her putting would have almost a Zen-like feeling. True, we worked on the usual—grip, posture, and alignment, but we always stressed visualization and feel, which would lead to much better technique. We also increased the amount of loft that Annika had on her putter to help her roll the ball better. Annika was a quick and willing student, always working longer and harder than I suggested, and always accepting the risks connected with change. The results she achieved gave me a great deal of satisfaction. She went from a two-victory season the year before we worked together to amassing a total of 30 wins over the next four years.

I was proud of her in 2003 when she entered the Bank of America Colonial in Fort Worth—a tournament I won in 1967, the first win of my PGA Tour career. Colonial Country Club, or "Hogan's Alley," as it is known, is a true shotmaker's course. Annika played spectacularly from tee to green, only to fail to putt as well as either of us would have hoped. Through all the pressure created by fans, media, and competitors, her confidence, smile, and competitive determination showed through.

I was very honored when she asked me to write this foreword because I understand what a powerful message her book contains for all golfers regardless of age or ability. Annika is a golfer in total control of all aspects of the game, especially when it comes to creative thinking. The goals she sets are no longer laughed at—such as total victories, single-season grand slams, and scores (she already owns a 59). She even speaks of

With Dave Stockton's help, I developed a much better "feel" for my putting stroke.

one day shooting a 54—all birdies. I wouldn't bet against her. Annika Sorenstam has become one of the most dominant female players in history. Let yourself learn from her here—her courage and strength, her determination and intelligence, and her deep faith in her ability. Then put it all to use in your own game, for your own improvement, and the results should be startling.

—By DAVE STOCKTON, *PGA Champion, 1970 and 1976*

Foreword

This must seem like a weird twosome—a singer writing a tribute to a golfer. But I had the pleasure of meeting Annika several years ago through a mutual friend, and since that first meeting we've spent some time together in each other's worlds. I have played golf with her—which is a totally amazing experience for a duffer like me—and she has been a great supporter of my music, coming to see my shows all over the place.

As brilliant as her golf is, it's only one of the things I admire about Annika. What really strikes me is the strength of her spirit—her determination to get better and better. I know what it takes to be at the top of your game, whether you're a doctor, a painter, a carpenter, a plumber, a singer, or a golfer. To be the best at anything, you have to be strong. You have to be willing to overcome all the obstacles that get in your way, and you have to make sacrifices. She's an athlete and I'm an entertainer, both of us blessed with talent, which is a gift. Annika has taken that gift and raised it to the highest level.

I'll never forget the 2003 Bank of America Colonial tournament, when Annika became the first woman in fifty-eight years to play in a PGA Tour event. Remember her opening tee shot? How wonderfully she hit the ball, straight and true. Then she gave a big smile, put her hand to her heart, and pretended to stagger away in relief. The pressure was incredible, but she still performed remarkably well, with grace and dignity, and she wasn't too proud to make fun of herself.

She wasn't trying to outdo the men that week. She was doing what she had done her whole life—challenging herself to reach the top of her potential. Annika was pushing Annika!

That's why I admire her so much. She will not allow herself to give a mediocre effort. She will not settle for second best. Annika believes in her dreams, and she follows them. She is an inspiration to me, and to millions of other men and women who are giving their all to reach their potential. I'm very proud to call her my friend.   —By CELINE DION

Prologue

I
n May 2003, I undertook the biggest challenge of my life—playing against the men of the PGA Tour at the Bank of America Colonial Tournament in Fort Worth, Texas. The timing couldn't have been better. I was peaking physically, mentally, and emotionally, coming off a season in which I'd broken or tied 30 LPGA records and won 13 times worldwide. Just two years earlier I couldn't have endured the physical challenge of being the first woman to play a PGA Tour event since Babe Zaharias in 1945, let alone a media frenzy that the great Babe could not have imagined.

While there was some criticism of my decision, I saw only the positives: the chance to take my game to a new level, to meet new people, to win new fans and, yes, to learn from the men of the PGA Tour. The worst that could happen would be to finish last—but even then I knew I would gain valuable experience.

When I woke on the morning of my first round, my stomach was jumping. I knew that every lesson I'd learned in golf and life would come into play that day. First and foremost, I had to face my fear—and, believe me, I was afraid. Television vans with satellite dishes lined the course, and there were so many fans—a record crowd of 40,000—that I employed Tiger Woods's security team for the week.

I saw the Colonial as my Mount Everest, and when I arrived at the course I briefly felt breathless, as if I really were about to climb a 29,000-foot peak. But the fans were overwhelmingly supportive and positive, as were my playing partners, Dean Wilson and Aaron Barber. I was touched when Dean arrived wearing a green "Go Annika" button: He and Aaron seemed as flustered as I was.

"I'm so nervous I don't know if I can handle this," Aaron told me, "but we'll go through it together."

I could barely feel my arms when we arrived on the 10th tee (our first of the day), but that's when my training as a competitive athlete kicked in. As the announcer

I was so nervous teeing off on Colonial Country Club's 10th hole (my first),
that relief flooded over me after my 4-wood split the fairway.

PROLOGUE

XIII

Here I am celebrating a birdie putt on the par-3 13th hole during the first round of the Bank of America Colonial—my first birdie on the PGA Tour.

introduced me, a different Annika took over. I drew a few deep breaths and began my preshot routine. Suddenly, despite the noise, energy, and excitement, there was solitude. My mind quieted. In some faraway sense I knew I was about to achieve everything I had ever worked toward, but I had just one thought as I stepped up to the ball: "Swing easy."

As soon as my 4-wood made contact, everything felt right. The ball hung in the air for what seemed an eternity, traveled 243 yards—and split the fairway. I'd faced the shot of my life and pulled it off. Relief flooded over me.

Although I didn't make the cut (a few more putts and I would have!), I'm proud that I pushed myself to the highest level. I did the best I could, and learned a lot along the way. But all the knowledge was just a fraction of what I've learned since I began playing the game as a shy 12-year-old in Sweden.

Now, I'm a shy 34-year-old—shy for a so-called celebrity at least. When I look back on my career, I realize how much golf has given me. It's taken me around the world and introduced me to interesting people, including my husband, David, who I met on a driving range. Golf has given me a home in Tahoe and a house in warm, sunny Florida, where I can practice year-round. Even more important, it has given me a way to master my abilities and challenge myself.

But no matter how often I win, or how many of my goals I meet, I'll never master the game itself. And I wouldn't expect to. Because golf is a never-ending challenge; there's always one more shot to hit, one more opponent to beat, one more course to think my way around. That's why I love the game, and I'll bet that's why you love it, too. And if my 22 years in golf have taught me anything, it's that we all need inspiration. I hope that by sharing what I've learned, I can help you climb your own Mount Everest— whether that means winning the U.S. Open, winning your club championship, or breaking 100 for the first time. Whatever your goal, I hope you discover—just like I did at the Colonial—that success isn't only about the goal you choose. It's about the experience, the effort, and the journey.

—By Annika Sorenstam

At

the Tee

MY JOURNEY · BACK TO BASICS

1 My Journey

GOLF—IT'S CHILD'S PLAY

It makes me laugh when people call me "robotic" or "mechanical." I might be all business on the course sometimes, but I'm smiling on the inside. I love the game of golf, and I've never lost the intense passion for sports and sense of pure fun I had as a kid. That passion helped turn a so-so junior player into an LPGA champion, and I've got my family to thank for instilling it in me at an early age.

I was born in 1970 in the small town of Bro, about 30 miles from Stockholm, where my father worked as a product manager for IBM and my mother worked at a bank until my sister Charlotta came along in 1973. We were typical middle-class Swedes in every way but one: We were sports crazy and super-competitive. My mother played golf while she was pregnant with me—I know I picked up the rhythm of her swing before I was born. And the only unusual thing about our three-bedroom house, which stood on a cul-de-sac, was the game room my dad had built in our basement. We had a badminton court, table tennis, and later, when Charlotta and I got interested in golf as teenagers, a hitting net. My fierce competitive drive was born in that rec room, during our family tournaments.

To my parents' credit, my first memories of golf have more to do with ice cream and pretend pony rides than with white-knuckle competition. In Sweden, middle-class people can afford to join golf clubs and kids are always welcome, so Charlotta and I tagged along with our parents to Viksjo Golf Club. When we were toddlers, we'd pretend their pullcarts were ponies and ride them. We were much more interested in fishing balls out of water hazards than with hitting shots. Back then, the most important part of a round was the ice cream we'd get at the 9th-hole snack shop.

As we got older, we'd putt on the practice green while my parents played. My parents

were—and still are—casual athletes. They never pushed us in sports. It was Charlotta and I who brought sports to a whole new level in our family.

When I first took up the game, I had no idea how important golf would someday be to me. Tennis seemed more exciting, and I spent my days dreaming about my idol, Bjorn Borg. He was the kind of champion I wanted to be. Not only was Bjorn a national hero, he dominated his sport. When he won Wimbledon in 1980 for the fifth time in a row, the country stood still, and everyone watched on television. What impressed me most was that Bjorn came from a middle-class background, like me. He didn't grow up with his own tennis court or fancy practice facilities. He would bang balls against his garage door. He proved that a person could achieve great things with talent and hard work.

I was pretty good at tennis, and attended camp every summer from age five to eleven. At 10, I was one of the top 10 players in Stockholm. I worked hard, but I just didn't *get* tennis. I didn't develop as quickly as I wanted. While I had a great forehand, my backhand was only so-so, and opponents learned to prey on that. I was too proud for that, so one day I tossed my racket in the closet and decided to give golf a try.

A new club had opened nearby, and Charlotta and I used to ride our bikes 20 minutes to get there. Today Bro-Balsta Golf Club has more than a thousand members, but then it was very small. We were among the first members, and Charlotta and I felt like family there. As teens we spent

Long before I was a golfer I was a fashion model. Here I am posing for some catalogue shots at ages 3 (left) and 4 (right).

Sports were important to my parents, but they always made sure my sister and I had fun in whatever we did. Here, on a family vacation to Leeds Castle in England, my father makes a game of pretend putting for me (middle) age 10, and Charlotta (far right), age 8.

Always together—Charlotta and I were close and competitive.

nearly every summer day at Bro-Balsta, playing a few holes, swimming in the lake, or hanging out at "Junior Corner," a shack near the driving range where we could play music and eat snacks. The club didn't have a ball picker, so in the evenings the pro would call Charlotta and me and offer to pay us to retrieve balls from the range. Then we'd say, "Well, we don't know, it's Friday night..." and negotiate until he'd raise the pay. We were paid about $10 a barrel to pick up thousands of balls, and it made our forearms strong. Usually the money went right back to the pro shop for balls, gloves, or a putter or two. When I got a little older

I worked in the shop, checking people in for their tee times, and sneaking outside to practice bunker shots when business was slow.

It took me a while to fall in love with the game. Like everyone who begins to play seriously, I was often frustrated. I threw my share of tantrums— you might say I was sometimes more John McEnroe than Bjorn Borg. At 12, my first handicap was 54, and my first clubs were a set of Mizunos that Charlotta and I shared. (She got the even-numbered clubs, I got the odds.) One day, out of sheer frustration over a poor shot, I grabbed the head of the 5-wood and slammed the club in the bag as hard as I could. I cracked the shaft near the grip. Knowing my father had worked hard to buy those clubs, I was so embarrassed that I kept playing with the club—you couldn't really see the crack—and finally had it reshafted when I'd saved enough money.

Today I'm known for my accuracy and mental strength under pressure, but my road to emotional and physical maturity in golf was a long one. It began with the Swedish National Golf Federation, and I was lucky that the Federation, like my parents, never lost sight of the fact that golf should be fun.

At age 16, I was getting better as a player, but I hadn't overcome my natural shyness.

NO SHORTCUTS!

I was a mediocre junior golfer. By 15, I was shooting in the mid- to high 90s, and no one would have said I was going places. But I was athletic and persistent, so I soaked up as much as I could in the organized practices run by the Swedish Federation. Junior golf begins at the club level, where pros work with juniors and recommend better players for Federation training camps. At first, the practices aren't too serious; they're a great way to hang out with friends. But soon the real work begins. Swedish players learn from an early age that the mind and body are inseparable, and both swing coaches and mental-game consultants guide better players from the youth program until the day they turn

pro. But the Federation also encourages athletes to think for themselves, which may be why so many Swedes are internationally successful.

At that age, I wasn't sure what I wanted to do with my life, but I began moving up through the Federation's ranks. I thought I was giving golf my all. Then, one evening, after a long day of play and practice, it started to rain. I called my father to pick me up. When he arrived, he looked silently out over the range, where a few juniors were hitting balls in the rain and dwindling light. On the ride home, my father said, "You know, Annika, there are no shortcuts to success."

Those words have affected everything I've done since that day. I think about them on mornings when I don't feel like getting out of bed to lift weights, when I'm not in the mood to practice after a tough round, and when I'm setting my goals at the beginning of each season. My father was right: If you don't push yourself as hard as you can, you'll never reach your potential.

I dedicated myself to practice that summer. Sometimes I hit balls until my hands ached, and I finally moved up from playing local to national tournaments. In the following year, 1987, I joined the Swedish National Team. That was the year I met a quiet, unassuming golf pro named Henri Reis.

Earlier that year the Swedish Federation held a district summer camp, choosing the best one or two girls from each club. I made the cut and Henri was my coach. I immediately was impressed by how he translated the complexities of the golf swing into simple language, and I saw instant results when I followed his advice. His course was just 20 minutes from my house, so once a week my parents would drop me off for a lesson, because it was vital for me to work with someone regularly. It was Henri's idea that I try a peculiar move I'm still known for today—turning my head toward the target before impact.

Was Henri blown away by my talent? Just ask him. He'll tell you that of all the young players he worked with, I never stood out. Other Swedes, including Carin Koch—now an LPGA star who to this day is still a good friend—were much better. At age 16, I loved golf, but I wasn't sure I could make it as a pro: I was shooting in the low 80s and hadn't broken par. Off the course, I was a math and computer enthusiast. I was considering becoming an engineer; sitting behind a computer suited my personality more than the very public life of a pro golfer. In school I never raised my hand, even when I knew the answers to teachers' questions. I could joke with people I knew well

(my sister was often the brunt of my antics— I used to make my friend Maria sit on poor Charlotta while I tickled her), but the thought of performing for a crowd of strangers made my palms sweat. I can't count the number of times I three-putted on the final hole of a tournament— on purpose—so that I wouldn't have to give a victory speech.

I thought the real reason for my three-putts— pure shyness—was my little secret. But some of the coaches were watching me and noticing my not-so-coincidental misses. So they announced that, at the next tournament, both the winner and the runner-up would have to give a speech. I figured, what's the point of finishing second if I had to face the crowd anyway.

In the fall of 1990, I made the 5,500-mile journey to the desert and the University of Arizona in Tucson.

I won that tournament and never looked back. The coaches' trick was a key to my maturity: I faced my fear and became better for it. But it was a lesson I would have to learn repeatedly— whether I was talking to the media or preparing to hit a tough shot. I also received some help from Pia Nilsson, a former LPGA player I met in the late 1980s when she worked with the Swedish National Team. Pia, like Henri, became part of my inner circle (see Chapter 11 for more information on her Vision54™ philosophy, which influences the way I play). She also was a frequent victim of my practical jokes. My favorite was the time a few of us players sprinkled itching powder on Pia's suit before the closing ceremonies at a tournament. She couldn't stop scratching that day—and we couldn't stop laughing.

With the Swedish National Team, I played junior tournaments in England, Portugal, Spain, and Italy. When I was 17, our team won the Junior European Championship, which brought me international attention. I had known that I was one of the better Swedish players, but that win gave me confidence. My increased prominence eventually led to an invitation to play in Japan, where the course of my life would change forever.

WORLD TRAVELER

After high school, I practiced and worked part-time answering phones in the Swedish PGA office. I wasn't yet a college student, but since I planned to enroll in the fall of 1989, I was asked—along with Robert Karlsson, who now plays on the European PGA Tour—to represent Sweden in a collegiate event in Tokyo. During a match against a player from the University of Arizona, I caught the attention of Kim Haddow, the Arizona coach. After the round, Kim asked if

Knickers were part of the uniform for the 1990 Junior World Championship in New Zealand.

The Swedish National Team, and coach Pia Nilsson (far left), were crucial to my development as a golfer.

I would like to play for Arizona on scholarship. I spent all of three seconds deciding.

I wasn't nervous going 5,500 miles from Sweden to Tucson, Arizona. I had traveled the world with the national team, hadn't I? But I was worried about being homesick.

My mother came to the rescue. Her last words as I boarded the plane were, "Remember, Annika, it's as far to come back as it is to go over." She was telling me I could always fly home.

When my flight landed in Tucson on a 100-degree August day, I thought there was a storm—there was heat lightning everywhere, but no rain. I headed to the freshman dorm and met my new roommate, Leta Lindley, who's now an LPGA player, too. Leta had a computer, a TV, and just about everything else a college student could want. I had my golf bag, a toothbrush, and a command of English that wasn't too impressive.

Culture shock set in when I couldn't remember the English words for simple things, like "blanket" and "pillow." Leta and her parents were incredibly nice. They took me shopping; I pointed and they interpreted.

I didn't take well to dorm life. I was a little older than most of the freshmen, and very independent. It was a party school, but for me the party began and ended on the course. While the other girls headed out for the weekend, I was hitting the sack after studying and practicing. Arizona golfers had so little free time that we usually spent Friday nights doing laundry.

I wanted to play against the best collegiate players, and being part of the Wildcats team was fun. But after years of being taught to think for myself, I disliked the restrictions set by the school and my coaches. We had tightly scheduled study periods and practices. Sometimes I had to raise

my hand just to go to the bathroom. But a couple of things made me feel better: Because I was older, I was soon allowed to move into an apartment; and I won my first tournament, the Oregon Invitational. I tied with another Wildcat, Debbie Parks, and we shared the trophy.

In my first college season, I finished out of the top 10 only once, and won the NCAA Championship by one stroke over Christy Erb from UCLA. Since I didn't grow up in the U.S., I didn't realize the win's importance until I returned as a sophomore and everyone was talking about it. During

my sophomore season I finished first four times and second three times in nine events. I ended that 1992 season as runner-up at the NCAA Championships behind the number-one college player in the country, Vicki Goetz.

That's when I decided to leave school. I was still working with Henri and Pia, and I wasn't learning much from my coach. I decided that I'd accomplished all I could in college: College Player of the Year in 1991, NCAA All-American in 1991 and 1992. I was ready for a larger arena. But before turning pro, I played the U.S. Women's

The greens were faster than anything I'd ever seen—I would have nine three-putts that week.

I was very impressed with the LPGA players. They dressed well, and had Tour golf bags and professional caddies. I got to hit balls on the range near Pat Bradley and Patty Sheehan, and I played a practice round with Meg Mallon. Everything was so routine for them—they went from the range to the putting green to the first tee. They didn't goof around like we did in college, and I realized that for them golf was a job. That week I finished as the second-lowest amateur, tying for 63rd—respectable, but no one was going to start calling Oakmont "Annika's Alley."

I spent the rest of the summer in an apartment in Phoenix, practicing for LPGA Qualifying School, which took place in Daytona Beach in October. I don't remember much about my rounds there—except for the suffocating pressure. It felt as if my future depended on every swing for four long days. Ultimately, I missed getting my LPGA card by one shot.

I was deeply disappointed and didn't know what this setback would mean for my career. The more I thought about it, though, the more I realized that things happen for a reason. Maybe I wasn't ready for the big leagues yet—maybe I needed to practice more. I decided to play in Europe for a while, but before I left I was invited to three LPGA tournaments in the spring. They would turn out to be harbingers of good things to come.

The 1993 PING/Welch's Championship in Tucson was played at Randolph Park North,

Amateur, where I lost in the finals to—you guessed it—Vicki Goetz. We were an exciting match-up, with my length balanced by her fabulous short game. It came down to the last hole, where I dunked a 6-iron shot in the water and lost by one stroke.

That was heartbreaking, but as runner-up I was invited to play in my first U.S. Women's Open, at the venerable Oakmont Country Club near Pittsburgh. To prepare I read up on Ben Hogan's win there in 1953—the year he almost won the Grand Slam. But my play was hardly Hoganesque.

where I'd played in college. Knowing the layout helped my nerves, and I tied for 38th and made $2,000. My next event, the Standard Register PING, was held at a desert gem near Phoenix called Moon Valley Country Club. For some reason the stars have always aligned for me at Moon Valley. I shot 66 in the second round and went on to my first top-10 finish as a pro—a fourth-place check worth $36,985. Overwhelmed, I called my father immediately with the news: In one week I had won more than I had budgeted to spend for the year!

At the next LPGA event I tied for ninth and won $8,264. I headed to the Ladies' European Tour knowing I had made the right career decision in turning pro.

PLAYING TO WIN

I finished second four times on the Ladies' European Tour in 1993, and was named Rookie of the Year. Now it was time for the big league: I joined the LPGA in 1994, after tying for 28th at Qualifying School. In my first two events I missed a cut and then tied for 72nd, but then came a string of top-20 finishes. I even came close to winning the Women's British Open, tying for second behind fellow Swede Liselotte Neumann. I was named LPGA Rookie of the Year in 1994, but I didn't have a professional victory yet, and was anything but famous.

I went into 1995 hoping to win an LPGA tournament and finish in the top 20 on the money list. Let's just say I exceeded my expectations. By the time I arrived at The Broadmoor, in Colorado Springs, for the 1995 U.S. Open, I was on a hot streak. I already had two wins in Europe and seven top-10 finishes on the LPGA Tour. There was something else, too: Just a month earlier, during the Evian tournament in

the French Alps, I'd gotten engaged.

I'd met David Esch in 1994 on the driving range of Moon Valley, where I was practicing for the Standard Register PING. David worked for PING, and he walked up to me and asked if I'd play a round of golf with him. We played one hole (he made birdie, I made par), and then I had to go—not because he won the hole, but because my mother had come to pick me up.

On our first real date, David took me to a Phoenix Roadrunners hockey game. That's where I discovered he was sports-crazy too. We were a great match.

We still are. When he proposed in France, I felt like all the pieces of my life were coming together. I became more relaxed on the course. David was with me at the '95 Open, and by Friday I led the tournament. By Sunday, though, I was five strokes behind Meg Mallon, tied for fourth with Pat Bradley. I was in the company of women far more experienced in the majors than I. But one thing I had learned is always to play as if you've got a chance to win.

After the first two holes on Sunday, Meg began to falter. She bogeyed the 3rd, then made triple bogey on the 6th. When I reached the 8th hole, we were both 1-under par. I made three more birdies and by the 14th I was ahead by three shots. When I realized my position, nerves set in. I bogeyed 15 and 16, then saved par on 17 after a chunked shot out of the rough. I made a routine par on 18 and then sat nervously in the NBC booth watching Meg finish. She was still at one under, and needed a birdie to tie me. And on the 18th green, she had a 15-foot putt to do just that. As I watched her take her putter back, my heart thumped as if it would explode.

Meg's ball stopped a foot left of the hole.

It took me a few seconds to realize what had happened: At age 24, in just my second year on tour, I had won my first LPGA tournament—and it was the U.S. Open! I called my parents in Sweden,

Golf in Sweden was so casual, I'd occasionally break out my jeans.

who had been listening to the broadcast on television after the satellite transmission went down and they lost the picture. They were crying, and soon I was crying, too. I was so astonished that I barely squeaked out "Thank you" at the awards ceremony. (I was still no good at victory speeches, despite my practice.) I hardly knew what to say to reporters at the press conference afterward—but I do remember saying I wasn't sure what I had gotten myself into. I was joking, but I had no idea how right that statement would be.

When I got home to Phoenix, my answering machine was full and my phone didn't stop ringing for days. I had never sought the spotlight. Now, I wanted to hide. I spent the next four days in bed, physically sick.

I wasn't lying around thinking, "poor me." I simply wasn't mentally prepared for such a big win. I wasn't used to having to say no to the media and to fans, but there were suddenly so many requests for my time—for autographs, interviews, appearances—that I could never have met them all. My life had been turned upside down, and I needed a break—to learn to see myself as a major winner.

I returned to competition at the Women's British Open, where I tied for second. I won two more tournaments and ended 1995 as the first player to lead the LPGA Tour, Ladies' European Tour, and Asian Tour money lists.

After a couple months off, 1996 started with as much promise as 1995 had ended. I finished second at the first major of the year, the Nabisco, then tied for 14th at our second major, the McDonald's LPGA Championship. I headed to Pine Needles in North Carolina for the U.S. Open two weeks later with the confidence of the defending champion. And, boy, did I play. I was

In 1996, I became the first foreign-born player to capture back-to-back U.S. Women's Open titles, winning by a comfortable six shots at Pine Needles.

one off the lead after the first round, led the tournament by three strokes after the second round, and maintained the three-stroke lead Saturday. On Sunday, I entered that magical zone where every shot goes where you want it to go. I birdied the 8th hole for a six-stroke lead. On the 10th I sank a 35-foot eagle putt. On the par-3 16th, my tee shot struck the pin. Another birdie. My parents watched proudly beside the 18th green as I finished my round, the gallery surging up the fairway behind me. I sank a six-foot par putt for a record-breaking score of 272, 8-under par.

Winning the 1995 Open had been incredible, but Meg Mallon's mistakes and bad luck had helped me that time. Now, a year later, no one else had even come close. Winning the 1996 Open secured my place in the history books. That was thrilling— and scary. An Open victory was something I had dreamed of for so long that winning my first still seemed unreal. Now I had won two of them.

Here, my husband David Esch and I are on our way to meet the King of Sweden at a 1997 royal gala.

SMILING ON THE OUTSIDE

I dominated the next two seasons in wins and earnings, but it would be five years before I won another major. Part of the reason was that after winning back-to-back U.S.Opens, I lost focus. I'd already reached my biggest goals—Player of the Year, the Vare Trophy (for the lowest LPGA scoring average), two U.S. Open titles. Lucky for me, Karrie Webb came along to give me a swift kick in the pants.

Karrie had been turning heads with her textbook swing since she won the 1995 Women's British Open a year before joining the LPGA Tour. In 1999 she won six tournaments, including a major. In 2000, I began to catch up, winning five times, but Karrie topped me on the money list with seven wins, including two majors.

In 2001, after getting some help from my friend Dave Stockton and practicing two hours a day in the off-season, my putting came together. I placed second in my first two events, and then won four in a row, including the Standard Register PING at Moon Valley, where I had the round of my life and became the first woman to break 60. (See Chapter 11 for plenty of details on my round of 59 that day.) That week I broke through to a new level as an athlete and as a public figure. I can't say I embraced the spotlight, but I no longer felt like running away from it.

Shooting 59 gave me tremendous confidence. The next week I ended my dry spell in majors, winning the Nabisco Championship. After the win, I made the traditional dive into the lake on 18 with an assist from my husband and sister.

The year ended with eight wins and six second-place finishes. I broke or tied 30 LPGA records, including lowest round (59), consecutive wins (four), largest come-from-behind victory (10

strokes at The Office Depot at Wilshire Country Club in Los Angeles), and surpassed $2 million in earnings. It was a great year, but as competitive as I am, I wanted to top it. But how?

My swing and putting stroke were sound, so the best way to improve was to get stronger and longer. You can learn more about that in Chapter 12. For now, it's enough to say that in 2002 I became nearly 15 yards longer off the tee.

It was the right tactic. By early July, I had six wins under my belt, including another Nabisco. I had fun that week, wearing bright red shoes on Sunday—they got almost as much attention as my play. I wanted to break Mickey Wright's record of 13 LPGA wins in one season. In the end I came close with 11, plus two wins overseas. It was a super year, and an exhausting one.

I'm someone who needs breaks between tournaments—especially after wins, when the media attention intensifies. In October and November of 2002, I played six weeks in a row and won three times. At the season-ending ADT Championship, where I battled Rachel Teske for the lead on Sunday, I kept thinking, "just four more holes... three more holes... two more holes." After that win I retired happily to our house at Lake Nona Country Club outside Orlando, where David and I had moved after we married in 1997. I needed a break from golf.

It's funny, but during the two best seasons of my career, I'd begun to cultivate interests outside the game. I'd always been interested in stocks and real estate, but cooking is my favorite escape. Whipping up a great pasta dish always erases any lingering frustrations from bogeys and missed putts. So in the winter of 2002–2003, I worked in the kitchen at Lake Nona Country Club, learning the basics of chopping, sautéing, and grilling. I even invited The

My red shoes got almost as much attention as my play at the 2002 Nabisco Championship.

Golf Channel to tape my amateur culinary moves. And suddenly the public part of my life started to be fun. The closer I got to reaching my potential, the more I could relax. People had always compared me to Nancy Lopez, saying I needed to be more outgoing. But I'm not Nancy and never will be. I'm simply too shy to take on that role. Still, I've started to give a little more of myself, to show my personality on and off the course.

When I accepted the biggest challenge of my

life and played against the men at the Bank of America Colonial in May 2003, I was able to wear my heart on my sleeve. Even under the toughest pressure and closest scrutiny, I was determined to have fun. I was smiling on the outside as well as the inside. If you face your scariest moment in public—on national TV—and survive, you're bound to be stronger and happier.

The Colonial gave me the confidence and focus I needed to complete the career grand slam. After claiming the McDonald's LPGA Champion-ship in July 2003 and then the Women's British Open that August, I had won every women's major at least once.

No one knows what the future holds. One day, when I can no longer compete at the highest level, I'll leave golf for other things—opening a restaurant, investing in the stock markets, raising a family with David. When that happens, I will miss golf, but I won't regret anything. I'll know that I gave the game my all—and loved every minute of it.

MY LIFE LESSONS

You may think of me as cool under pressure, an athlete willing to take risks and brave the consequences. But I wasn't born that way. I spent years learning the tactics that have helped me become a champion.

I've simplified my favorite lessons to share them with you. They're as effective in real life as they are on the course.

- **Face your fear:** Golf involves psychological fear—of hitting poor shots, looking foolish, or losing your ball in a water hazard. It's best to accept that fear and tackle it head-on. In practice, focus on the shots and situations that make you nervous or afraid until your fear is replaced with confidence.

- **Learn from everything:** I try to see every situation, good or bad, as a learning experience. At the 2002 British Open, an event I desperately wanted to win, I got overexcited because I wanted to play so well—and I missed the cut. I learned to treat majors like any other tournament. When you learn from every situation, your confidence grows.

- **Take one shot at a time:** This is one of the most important concepts of all. For each shot, you must let go of positive and negative emotions and focus on the task at hand: making the best swing that you possibly can. You're going to feel angry after bad shots, and elated after exceptional ones; accept those feelings and quickly move on. A consistent preshot routine (see Chapter 3) can help you stay in the moment.

- **Focus on what you can control:** Golf is a game of skill and luck. No matter how well you play, someone else might play better. No matter how solid your swing, your ball may bounce into a terrible lie. In golf, as in life, there's no sense fuming over things you can't control. Use your energy thinking about and working on what you can change.

- **There are no shortcuts:** Golf can be frustrating at times, and improvement comes only with time and hard work. Once you accept that there are no quick fixes, you'll get more out of the game: You'll get the satisfaction that comes from working hard at something rewarding.

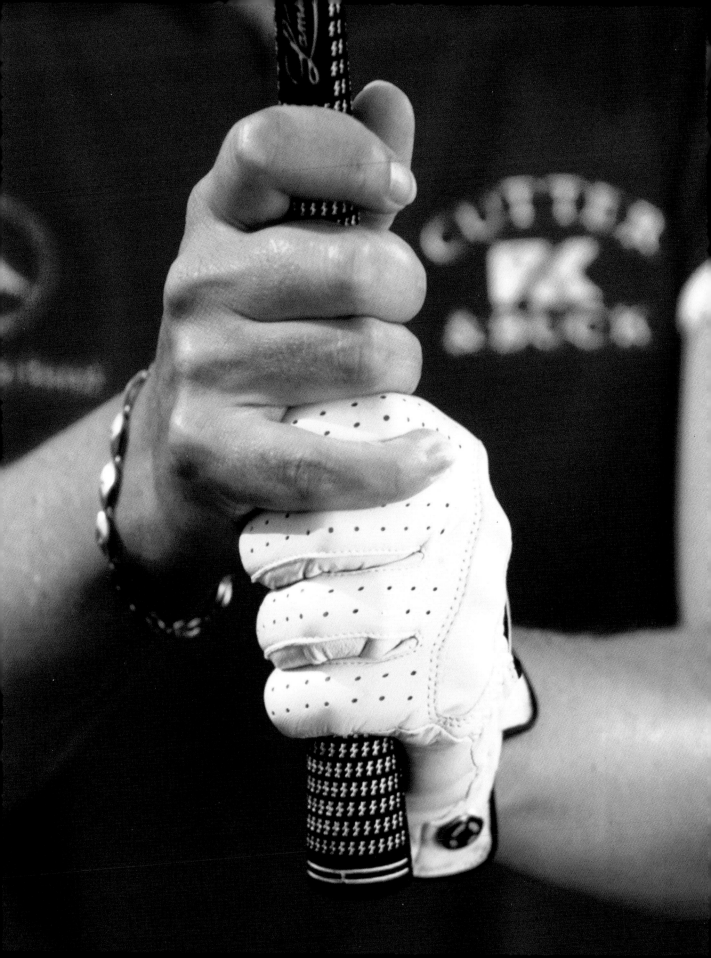

Back to Basics

FUNDAMENTALS FOR EVERY SWING

If you catch me on the practice range at an LPGA event, chances are you'll see me hitting balls with a shaft lying on the ground in front of my toes, pointing toward the target. I'm checking my alignment, making sure that I'm properly aimed. I do this every time I practice, whether I'm at home or on the road. And as you walk down the range, you'll probably see other players doing the same thing.

Yes, even the best players in the world have to monitor the fundamentals—grip, posture, and alignment—on a regular basis. I know that when I get off-track, it's very rarely a swing problem. The mistake is usually made before I take the club back.

During the first two days of competition at the 2003 Solheim Cup in my home country of Sweden, I was losing every ball to the right. I was lucky that my coach, Henri Reis, was on hand. Henri saw that my alignment was off, and we corrected it after Saturday's four-ball matches. In Sunday's singles—the Solheim version of the Super Bowl—I hit the ball better than I had all week to defeat Angela Stanford of the United States 3 and 2 and help Europe recapture the Cup. It was a simple adjustment— my body was aimed too far to the right and Henri got me to square up to the target— but it might have made the difference between winning and losing in the biggest team event in women's golf.

Henri travels to the United States every six weeks or so during the tournament season so we can review my grip, posture, and alignment. These are the foundations of the swing he and I worked on from the beginning, when I was a teenager just learning how to play this game. It is because of these building blocks that I'm able to repeat my swing again and again, consistently delivering under pressure.

LET YOUR FINGERS DO THE GRIPPING

I'm known as one of the game's most accurate players. But I'm only as good as my grip. Ben Hogan wrote, "Good golf begins with a good grip," because after all, your grip is the only connection you have to the club. How you place your hands on the club goes a long way toward determining the position of the clubface at impact, what direction the ball takes, and how much power you produce. Every golfer wants power and accuracy. But how many golfers pay enough attention to the grip?

Should you hold the club in your palms? Absolutely not. The fingers provide all the power and control you need. Picture holding the club in your fingers as if you were throwing a baseball (I'm demonstrating here with a golf ball). Using your fingers allows your wrists to hinge and unhinge during the swing, creating extra speed through impact. This extra snap through the ball is what separates pros from most golfers. Amateurs generally hold the club more in the middle of their hands, which limits this hinging action. The result is less distance.

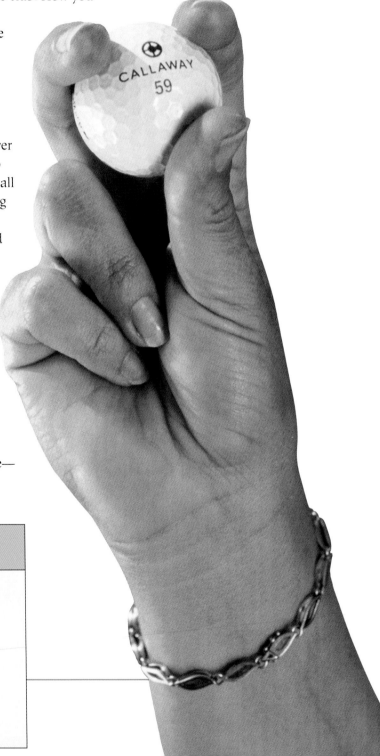

LEFT-HAND GRIP: "THE SIXTH FINGER"

Most beginners use a weak left-hand grip— with the hand rotated to the left on the handle— and therefore have a hard time squaring the

ATTENTION LEFT-HANDERS

I must apologize to all you left-handed golfers. Like the vast majority of players, I am right-handed, and the terms I use are for right-handed golf. If you are a lefty, simply substitute "left" for "right" and vice-versa when reading my advice.

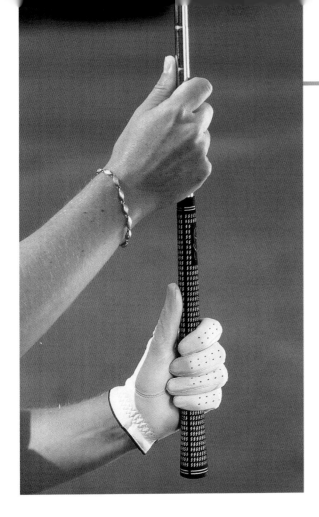

To ensure a good left-hand grip, hold the club verti-
cally in front of you with your right hand on the shaft,
then add your left (*left*). Rest the grip diagonally
along the base of your fingers, from a point just
below your left pinkie to the first knuckle on your left
index finger (*below*). The club should sit securely
under the fleshy part in the heel of your hand.

end of the club should sit under the heel pad,
which my coach likes to call "the sixth finger."
(Why is it like a finger? Because if you took the
last three fingers of your left hand off the grip,
you could still balance the club comfortably
under the heel pad.)

With the club resting comfortably in your
fingers, wrap your thumb over the grip so that
the fat part of your heel pad sits on the center of
the grip and the base of your thumb touches the
tips of your middle fingers. Now you're ready to
add the right hand.

Never thought the grip could be so complicated? Don't worry... we're almost there. All
that's left is to add your other hand.

clubface at impact. They typically miss to the
right because the clubface is open (pointing to
the right) at impact.

To improve a weak grip, hold the club in front
of you with your right hand on the shaft, and
place the fingers of your left hand on the grip.
Rest the grip diagonally along the base of your
fingers, from the top of your hand's heel pad to
the first knuckle on your index finger. The butt

Grip the club in the same manner you would a
baseball or other small ball—in your fingers (*left*).
The more it rests in your fingers, the easier it is to
hinge and unhinge your wrists, creating additional
clubhead speed through the ball.

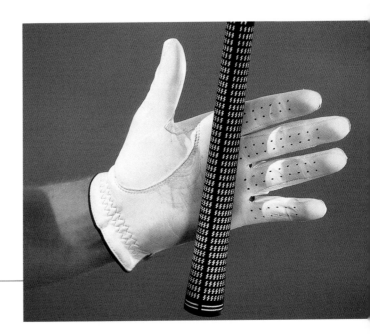

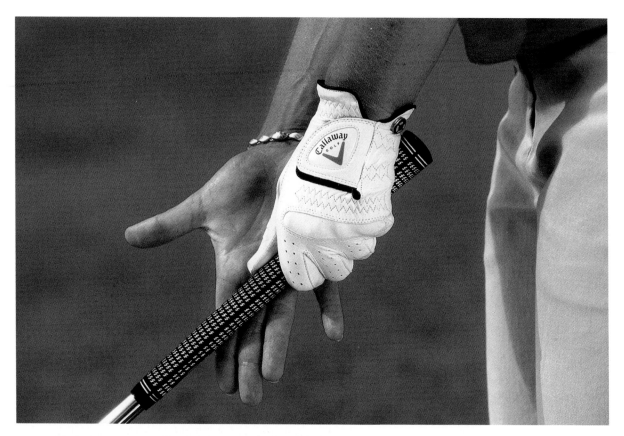

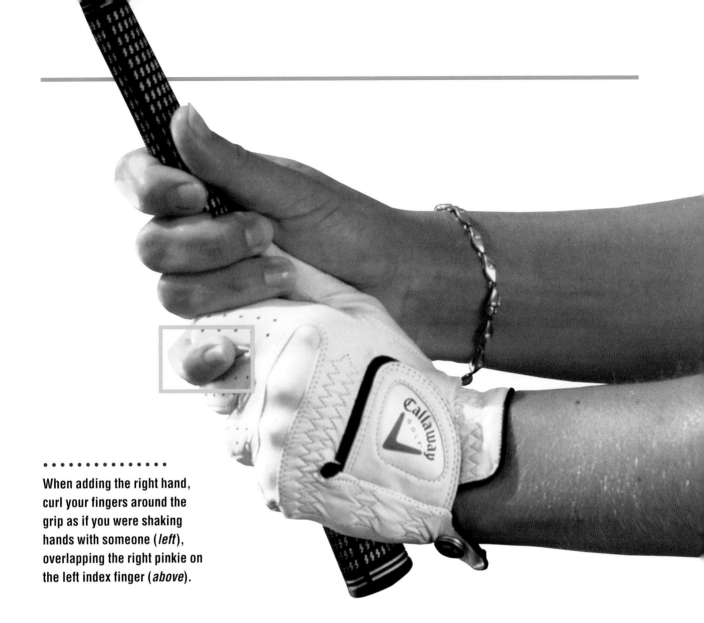

When adding the right hand, curl your fingers around the grip as if you were shaking hands with someone (*left*), overlapping the right pinkie on the left index finger (*above*).

RIGHT-HAND GRIP: SHAKE HANDS

While most beginners set their left hand too weak, they do the opposite with their right hand. They rotate their hand clockwise, so it sits almost under the grip. That's asking for trouble.

Instead, make sure your right palm faces the target. Rest the club along the base of your middle two fingers (*opposite page, top*) and close your hand, curling your fingers around the grip as if you were shaking hands with someone (*opposite page, bottom*). This is a good reminder to yourself that the club should be held in your fingers, not your palms. Your right index finger and thumb should nearly touch, and your right pinkie should overlap the left index finger—this is commonly called the Vardon, or overlapping grip. The base of your right thumb sits snugly over your left thumb, with the lifeline of your right hand applying gentle pressure to your left thumb (*above*).

LEAVE IT
IN NEUTRAL

I use a neutral grip, in which the Vs formed by the thumbs and index fingers of each hand point between my chin and right shoulder. This helps me get the clubface square at impact—to the clubhead's original address position. If you struggle with a slice, you may want to strengthen your grip some, so the Vs point more toward your right shoulder. That's the grip I began with as a junior, but I hit a lot of low hooks with it. I weakened my grip as I learned more about my golf swing.

At address, my palms face each other, with the right palm pointing to the target. This is important, since the right palm mirrors the position of the clubface throughout the swing. If it's open (pointing right of the target) or closed (pointing to the left) at address, I must make some compensation during the swing to square the clubface at impact. And doing that is a tall order even for the best players in the world.

• • • • • • • • • • • • • • • • • • • •

I prefer a neutral grip, in which the Vs created by the thumb and index finger of each hand point between my chin and right shoulder (*right*). In a strong, anti-slice grip, the Vs point more toward the right shoulder.

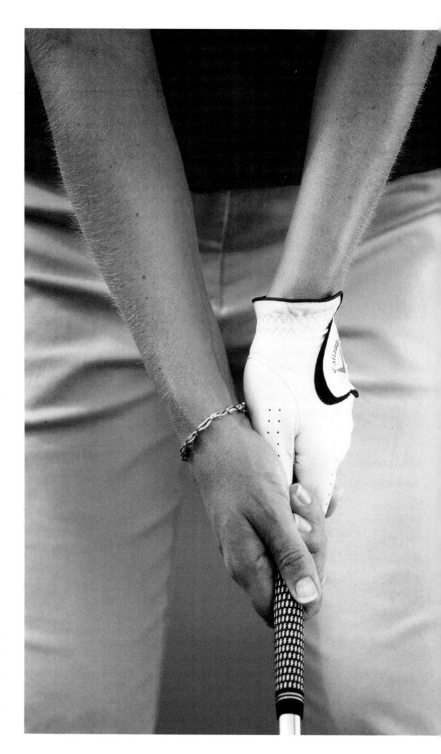

POSTURE: YOU'RE AN ATHLETE

A good grip is the first step toward good golf. The next step is posture. Your posture determines the size and shape of your swing.

I like to use the word "athletic" to describe my posture, because I think of myself as an athlete. I spend about as much time in the gym as most professional team sport athletes do, and I'm in the best physical shape of my life (see Chapter 12 to learn more about my fitness regimen). I'm getting stronger all the time, and that's important when you're playing 72 holes in four days, or 54 in three. You need to maintain your concentration and energy for every hole.

At address, I stand like a boxer ready to throw a jab—or receive one (*left*). My weight is on the balls of my feet, and my knees are slightly bent. I could move in any direction, like a shortstop or a tennis player waiting for a serve. My body is in a state of readiness.

At address, I stand
like a boxer
ready to throw a
jab—or receive one.

STANCE: THE RIGHT TILT

There are two fundamental tilts: You tilt your spine away from the target, and tilt your upper body toward the ground. The first tilt is a function of the grip: Since my right hand is lower on the handle than my left, my right shoulder needs to be lower. This tilt positions my upper body behind the ball, making it easier for me to load my weight onto my right side. From here, my weight will naturally want to shift forward, swinging the club on the proper inside-out path to the ball.

If my weight shifts forward at the top of the backswing—what is commonly referred to as a reverse weight shift—it has no place to go but backward on the downswing, which makes it hard to get any power behind the shot. That's why it's so important to load up on your right side, as it triggers the correct forward motion in the downswing.

• • • • • • • • • • • • • • • • • • • •

Tilt your spine away from the target so your right shoulder is lower than your left. This matches the position of your hands on the grip, setting your upper body behind the ball.

STANCE: BUTT OUT

Have you ever noticed how a boxer never throws a punch standing straight up? He's bending forward from the hips with his knees flexed. Why? Because that's how he gets leverage for his punches. The same holds true for a golfer. To swing the club with force, you need to maintain a consistent forward tilt toward the ground.

To establish this tilt, I bend forward from the hips about 30 degrees, sticking my butt out as if I were taking a seat on the edge of a bar stool. This "sit-down" position creates the perfect counterbalance between my upper and lower body, and straightens my spine so I can make a full shoulder turn.

The "butt-out" tilt also puts me the correct distance from the ball. My shoulders hang in line with my toes—not in front of them—and my arms are relaxed. If my arms are tense, it's a good indication that I'm standing either too close or too far away from the ball.

• • • • • • • • • • • • • • • • •

Bend forward from your hips, pushing your butt out as if you were taking a seat on the edge of a bar stool. Your back should be relatively straight—not rounded— which allows you to turn your shoulders freely to the top.

GRIP TEST: A SHOW OF HANDS

Are you the right distance from the ball? Here's how to check: Take your right hand off the club and let it hang by your side. Your palm should hang so that when you move it back into place, it fits your left hand without any twisting or repositioning. If your hand moves behind the grip when you return it to the club, you're standing too far away; if it moves in front, you're too close.

To see if you're standing the correct distance from the ball, take your right hand off the club and let it hang by your side. Then move it back into place. It should fit your left hand; if it doesn't, you're standing too close or too far away.

If your back is rounded, there's no room for your arms to swing…

Hold a shaft to your back to get a feel for the correct angle in your spine at address.

MIRROR, MIRROR

Find a mirror in your home or on the practice range. Hold a club against your back so that the grip-end sits on your tailbone and the shaft points up your spine. Make sure that the shaft stays in contact with your back. If you can maintain this same straight angle throughout your full swing, your shoulders will turn at right angles to your spine, moving the club on-plane and creating maximum clubhead speed. If your back is rounded, there's no room for your arms to swing, and you'll have trouble staying in your original posture.

FOOT BALLS

My posture isn't complete until my weight is evenly distributed over the balls of my feet. This encourages good balance throughout the swing and helps my arms swing more freely. But many amateurs set up with their weight on their toes, which forces them to dip their heads and front shoulders during the backswing, throwing their swings completely off-balance.

Can you find the balls of your feet? Here's how:

Your weight should be evenly distributed over the balls of your feet. To find these balance points, raise yourself up on your toes…

Hold a club straight up and down in front of your chest with your knees locked and feet shoulder-width apart, then raise yourself up on your toes. Slowly lower the clubhead and your feet to the ground, flexing your knees. You'll soon find the balls of your feet—because the slightest weight shift toward the heels or toes will cause you to lose your balance.

• • • • • • • • • • • • • • • • • •

...then slowly lower your feet to the ground, flexing your knees. The slightest shift in weight toward your toes or heels will throw you off-balance.

ALIGNMENT: GET THE SHAFT

You may have the perfect grip, posture, and swing, but if you're lined up 20 yards to the right of the target, that's where you're going to hit the ball. It's crucial to check your alignment as often as you can.

Put a club or umbrella on the ground between the ball and your feet, with the clubshaft parallel to your target line. Now step in behind the club and build your stance, using the shaft as a guide to aim your entire body. Whenever you change targets, move the club.

ROUTINE: FACE FIRST

As I set up over a shot, the very first thing I do is aim the clubface at my target, whether the target is a flagstick, a tree in the distance, a bush, or the edge of a bunker. Then I build my stance around my aim, aligning my body—shoulders, hips, knees, and feet—on a parallel plane to the left of the target line.

If you take your stance before you aim the clubface—a common mistake—you'll probably aim your body at the flag, which will point the clubface well right of the target. This is the most common alignment fault among amateurs—aiming too far to the right—and the only way to compensate is to swing over the top or turn the hands over and hook the ball. Aim correctly and you won't have to jump through hoops trying to hit the ball straight.

• •

Get in the habit of aligning yourself correctly by practicing with a shaft on the ground (*left*). On the course, make sure to aim the clubface first before taking your stance (*right*).

STANCE: YOUR
SUPPORT SYSTEM

At address, you want to create a solid foundation that can support the swinging motion of your arms and upper torso. That's why the width of your stance is so important. The longer the club, the longer the swing's arc and the wider you must spread your feet. The shorter the club, the smaller the arc, and the closer your feet should be to each other.

The longer the club, the wider my stance. With the driver, my heels are even with the outsides of my shoulders (*left*); for a 5-iron, they're in line with my armpits (*above*); for a wedge, even closer together (*right*).

With the driver, my heels are even with the outsides of my shoulders. That's wide enough to support the clubhead speed generated by a long club with a wide swing arc. With a mid-iron, my heels are in line with my armpits, and with the short irons and wedges, my heels are even closer together—lined up with the logos on the front of my shirt.

Notice that both my feet are flared out a bit. That allows my hips to turn freely, so I can

generate more power and square the clubface. If your right foot is perpendicular to the target line at address, it restricts you from making a full hip turn.

BALL POSITION: WOODS FORWARD, WEDGES BACK

My ball position varies, depending on the length of the club. With a driver, I play the ball just inside my left heel. This promotes an ascending blow at impact, which helps get the ball airborne. With my fairway woods and long irons, I play the ball between the middle of my stance and my left heel. With my mid-irons, the proper position is a ball-length or two forward of center. And with my short irons and wedges, I play the ball in the center of my stance, below my sternum. Try these variations—you might be surprised how much ball position at address can influence the shots you hit.

WEDGE

. . . .

The length of the club also dictates ball position. With my short irons and wedges, I play the ball in the center of my stance, below my sternum (*left*); for my mid-irons, one or two balls forward of center (*opposite page, right*); for my driver, just inside my left heel (*opposite page, left*).

CHECKPOINT: LOOK TO YOUR FOREARMS

Because your arms swing along the same path as your shoulders, it's critical that you align your shoulders correctly. That's why, after aiming the clubface, I start aligning my body from the top down, starting with my shoulders and working down to my feet.

Because it's very hard to see where my shoulders are pointed at address, I look to the fronts of my forearms to see if they're parallel to the target line. If my arms are hanging naturally, my forearms will be on the same line as my shoulders. You can check this by having someone hold a shaft up against your forearms—as my coach is doing here—and then stepping away to see if the shaft is parallel to the target line. It's a great way to train your shoulders to set up square to the target.

• •

Look to your forearms to see whether your shoulders are aligned correctly. Have someone hold a shaft against your forearms, as my coach Henri Reis is doing here, and then step away to see if your arms and shoulders are square to your target.

ANNIKA'S FUNDAMENTAL KEYS

If I'm not hitting the ball as straight as I'd like, the first thing I check is my alignment. If that's okay, then I move on to my grip and my posture. I don't try to change my swing; instead I revisit my fundamentals. If I get these right, I'll have an excellent chance of hitting the ball exactly where I want it to go.

- Hold the grip more in the fingers of both hands and less in the palms.
- The Vs formed by your thumbs and index fingers should point between your chin and right shoulder.
- Tilt your spine away from the target so your right shoulder is lower than your left, mirroring the position of your hands on the club.
- To set up the proper distance from the ball, bend from your hips, pushing your butt out as if you were sitting on the edge of a bar stool.
- Aim the clubface directly at your target, then align your body parallel to the target line.

The Full

....

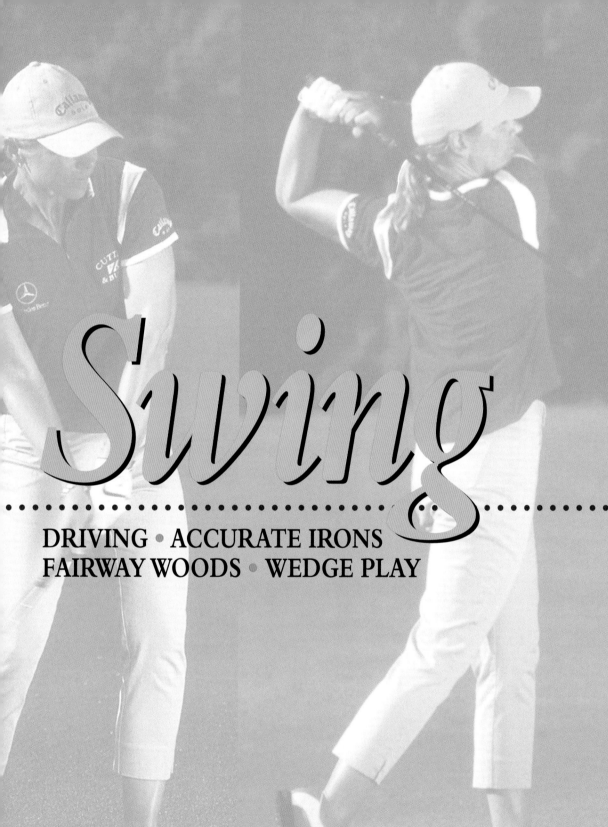

Swing

DRIVING • ACCURATE IRONS
FAIRWAY WOODS • WEDGE PLAY

Driving

HIT IT LONGER AND STRAIGHTER

The tee shot is the most important shot in golf. If you're in the trees or the rough all day, you're going to struggle to score. That puts pressure on the rest of your game, and that's why I place so much emphasis on driving. I know that if I can consistently keep the ball in the short grass, I'll make my share of birdies.

On the tee, I feel totally at ease with my driver. I trust that I can keep the ball in play, and that gives me the confidence to air it out when I need to. I had that confidence as I stood over my final drive at the 2003 Weetabix Women's British Open. At the time, both Se Ri Pak and I were tied at 10-under par. It had been pretty much a two-horse race since the start of the back nine, with Se Ri, the 2001 champion, having birdied No. 16 to draw even. There was a tremendous amount riding on this tee shot: If I could find a way to win, not only would I capture my first British Open, but I would become the sixth female pro to complete the career Grand Slam.

Se Ri played first to the par-4, 371-yard 18th hole at Royal Lytham and St. Annes Golf Club, and hit into a deep fairway bunker. From there, I knew she'd do well to make par, so I felt a birdie would win. At first I considered hitting a 7-wood, but that would have left me with an extremely long approach shot. It had to be driver.

I set up for a slight draw, figuring that if I hit the ball dead straight I'd be clear of any bunkers. Standing over the ball, I told myself: *You've hit this shot before. Just focus on what you've got to do.* Sure enough, I released the club perfectly and ripped it down the middle. To this day, I can still feel the ball compressing against the center of the clubface. That was one of the best drives I've ever hit.

Moments later, after Se Ri made bogey and I made par, I had my Grand Slam.

EFFORTLESS POWER

Since 1998, I've gained more than 23 yards off the tee—raising my driving average from 246.8 yards in '98 to 270 yards in 2003. That's quite a leap, going from the middle of the LPGA pack in driving distance to No. 1 in five short years. Most of these gains are due to my Callaway Golf equipment and improved fitness—I'm much stronger now than I used to be—which I'll detail later in the book. Ten years ago, I was lucky to hit one out of four par-5 holes in two shots; today I can reach 75 percent of the par-5s in two. On par-4s, I'll often hit an 8-iron into the green while other players are hitting 6-irons. That's a huge advantage. And I'm as accurate as ever off the tee, which is what I'm proudest of. It's great to hit it far, but if you hit it far into the woods, who cares?

Despite my newfound strength, my swing is pretty much the same as it was during my rookie season in 1994. I don't try to hit the ball any harder now. Sure, my clubhead speed has increased, but I still swing my driver with the same rhythm and tempo. That's the single biggest key to hitting the ball farther. When I'm swinging well, I make little effort to hit the ball. It feels like I'm rotating my body and the ball just gets in the way.

• •

My best drives, like this famous 4-wood on the 10th tee at the Bank of America Colonial in 2003, occur when I swing effortlessly. I try to hit all of my clubs—from my sand wedge to my 5-iron to my driver—with the same easy rhythm and tempo. If I swing too hard, my tempo quickens and my accuracy suffers.

DON'T BREAK YOUR SPEED LIMIT

I make the same swing with all my clubs, whether it's my driver, 5-iron, or sand wedge. If I want to hit the ball farther, I just grab a longer club. Of course, my driver swing doesn't look like my wedge swing, because the driver's shaft is longer and the swing's arc is bigger, but rarely do I try to swing my driver harder. When I do, the ball usually goes sideways.

If my caddie, Terry McNamara, sees my tempo getting quick, he reminds me to "swing-

six." On a scale of 1 to 10, 6 is my speed limit with the driver. Any more than that and I start to lose control.

I suggest that you find a tempo that allows you to swing under control. Swing harder than 6 if you like, as long as you can maintain your balance. You should finish with your weight on the outside of your front foot and your back foot on its toes. If you're falling over, you won't hit the ball solidly or keep it in play.

RATE YOUR FINISH

If you finish in balance, with your body in a pretty straight line over your front foot (*below*), chances are you were balanced during the swing. The next time you play, rate your finish position from 1 to 10 on each drive—1 for falling over, and 10 for perfect balance. If you're averaging less than 7, you're probably swinging too hard.

This drill was devised by Pia Nilsson, former coach of the Swedish National Team. It will get you thinking about balance, which will help you keep the ball in the fairway.

WATCH AND LEARN

If you're struggling with your tempo—particularly if you're moving too quickly— watch the easy swings of Tour players like Ernie Els and Fred Couples. Then try to mimic their smooth, relaxed tempo when you play.

It worked for me. My biggest fault at an early age was that I often failed to make a complete backswing turn. I was too fast with my hips. Watching other players with a beautiful flow and rhythm to their swings convinced me to slow down.

ON THE RANGE: FIND YOUR RHYTHM

While warming up on the range before a round, I start by reaching for my 60-degree wedge. I hit a few wedge shots to get loose and find my timing, and then proceed to short irons and longer clubs. Before I bust out the driver, however, I reach again for my lob wedge (*left*). Why? Because swinging a few wedges keeps my tempo relaxed and smooth when I get to the driver. I want to swing the driver with the same ease that I do my wedges, because I'll connect better and hit it farther—not to mention *a lot* straighter.

Most amateurs head to the range and immediately grab the driver. Then they hit about a dozen balls, swinging as hard as they can. That's the tempo they take with them on the course—too fast.

So keep your swings smooth on the range. Remember, the driver is designed to hit the ball far—it's the longest club in your bag and has the

Most amateurs head to the range and immediately grab the driver. Then they hit about a dozen balls, swinging as hard as they can. That's the tempo they take with them on the course—too fast.

least amount of loft. You don't have to kill it. Just make a smooth swing. You'll be surprised how far the ball goes.

• •

Warming up before a round, I'll start with my lob wedge and gradually progress to the longer clubs in my bag. But before I hit driver, I'll loosen up with the lob wedge again. This encourages me to swing my driver at the same easy tempo as my wedge.

TAKEAWAY: ALL TOGETHER NOW

When I say smooth, I don't mean throttle your motion all the way back; you still have to hit the ball. I just mean *unhurried*. Many amateurs are so anxious to hit the ball that they jerk the club back, then start down from the top just as fast. But you don't want to use up all of the club's speed before impact. You want to build speed gradually, so the clubhead is moving its fastest when it gets to the ball.

To make sure my swing gets off to a smooth start, I take the club back with my hands, arms, shoulders, and hips all moving in unison (*above*).

In this one-piece action, the larger muscles of my body move the club back the first 18 inches or so. This starts the club back on the correct path— just inside the target line—promoting the wide, circular arc I want with the driver.

Most high-handicappers start the swing with their hands, snatching the club well to the inside, which promotes a narrow arc and a steep downswing. To keep your swing together, pretend that your hands are in cement as you start the backswing with your arms, shoulders, and hips.

WAGGLE YOUR TENSION AWAY

Most pros use some type of waggle in their preswing routines. Some do it to pre-set the correct swing path, while others—like me—do it to promote a smooth, flowing takeaway and a good shoulder turn. In my waggle, I lift the clubhead straight up and down several times before pulling the trigger, pulling my arms into my body. The clubhead barely grazes the ground. This helps relieve any tension I may have in my shoulders. Now my arms feel soft and my grip pressure is light. My grip is firm enough to hold the club, but soft enough to let me feel the weight of the clubhead and shaft. Now I'm ready to swing.

Before pulling the trigger, I'll gently bob the club-head up and down several times, making sure not to ground the club. This pre-swing waggle helps relax my arms and shoulders, promoting a smooth takeaway and a full shoulder turn.

BACKSWING: ON THE LEVEL

Early in my career I spent a lot of time working on my backswing, training myself to make a complete turn behind the ball. This is critical to my tempo: The better the turn, the more time I have to swing the club down from the top. Instead of rushing the club, I can start down slowly.

If I have a swing flaw, it is that I sometimes lift my arms too much in the backswing. This throws my whole backswing out of whack—my right hip lifts and my left shoulder drops, shifting my weight toward the target instead of behind the ball.

Now, my weight has no place to go but back if I want to get behind the ball at impact. Result: I block the ball out to the right.

To make a better backswing, I think about keeping my shoulders nearly level, as if I were steadying the wings of an airplane. This lets my right hip rotate straight back without lifting. With my right hip fully turned, I can complete my shoulder turn to the top. My left shoulder moves under my chin, helping to square the clubface. From here, all I do is let my body unwind and rotate through the shot. My weight transfers easily, setting up the proper inside path to the ball.

Turn—don't lift—your shoulders to the top, as if you were trying to steady the wings on an airplane.

HIP TO BE SQUARE

On the backswing, try to turn your hips within an imaginary cylinder the width of your stance. Don't let your right hip slide past your right foot. To train my hips to move this way, I sometimes practice with an umbrella or shaft angled into the ground so it's just touching my right hip at address. The object is to turn my right hip without bumping the umbrella (or shaft).
If my hip sways, it will move the umbrella. But if I can turn without pushing the umbrella, I've made the right move. You can bet my driver will be square to the ball at impact.

TRANSITION: EASY FROM THE TOP

May 22, 2003: Colonial Country Club, Fort Worth, Texas. My chance to make history.

I don't think I've ever been as nervous as I was on the 10th tee at Colonial. There was so much buildup to that shot, so many people watching—thousands at the course and millions more on TV—that I don't know how I took the club back, let alone hit the fairway. I felt sick to my stomach, my hands were sweaty—everything you feel when you're under heavy stress. And it didn't help that I was hitting last in my group. It was a horrible feeling. I could have easily heeled it into the crowd.

On the tee, I had just one swing thought and that was to take it easy from the top. Like many golfers, I have a tendency to come over the top when I hurry the downswing. When this happens, my right shoulder comes forward instead of dropping straight down, which throws the club on a steep, out-to-in path. If I start the downswing slowly, my hands,

arms, and body have a better chance to stay connected (*below*). Then I can release and square the clubface with my arms and body, instead of relying on my hands to time the release perfectly. If your hands and arms outrace your body, or vice versa, it's very difficult to square the face consistently—especially under pressure.

Take it easy from the top. I carried that one swing thought with me the entire first round, and it worked like a charm. I hit all but one fairway

and 14 of 18 greens in regulation, and the four I missed were near-misses. Under the circumstances, it was the best ball-striking round of my career.

•••••••••••••••••••••••••••••••

I carried only one swing thought with me during the first round at the Colonial: Take it easy from the top. It worked beautifully, as I hit all but one fairway under the most intense pressure I've ever faced.

NOW YOU SEE IT, NOW YOU DON'T

One question I'm always asked is, "What are you looking at during impact?" To be honest, I have no idea. Really. It's not the ball, that's for sure. On television, it appears as if I'm looking at the target, unsure of where I'm going. But that's not it, either. My head just follows my shoulders. As I swing through, my head turns along with my body, both releasing to the target simultaneously.

This may look unusual, but for me it has become my signature move. After impact, it feels like the club, my body, and even my head are all chasing the ball toward the target.

• •

My signature move: As I swing through impact, my head and shoulders release toward the target simultaneously, as if they're chasing after the ball. It looks unusual, but it's quite effective.

IT'S OKAY TO LOOK UP

I often hear amateurs murmur, "Keep your head down!" after a poor shot. But that's a myth. If your head is glued in place throughout the swing, you have to be made of rubber to get your chest and shoulders through to the target.

It's okay to look up to see where the ball is going! Just make sure your head continues to rotate forward. By unlocking your head, you'll allow your shoulders to turn on a more level plane and your hips to rotate naturally toward the target, accelerating the club through impact.

IMPACT DRILL

GET A HEAD START

This move originated as a drill my coach Henri Reis taught me as a junior to help eliminate my "reverse-C" finish. I had a tendency to hit off my back foot, so much so that my back would arch away from the target at the finish, instead of finishing in a straight line. To get me to shift my weight to the left during the downswing, he had me hit balls while turning my head to the target *before* impact.

At first, it felt pretty weird. But then I noticed how my weight was no longer staying on my right leg—and how I was starting to hit the ball much better. After a while, Henri said, "You've got the hang of it," and he told me to switch back. Naturally, I fell into my old habit again, so I went back to the drill until it became second nature. It worked so well at getting rid of my reverse-C that I made it part of my normal swing.

Try Henri's drill yourself—particularly if your weight tends to fall back at impact and you make inconsistent contact. Start by hitting some wedges (*right*), letting your eyes track forward at impact instead of trying to keep your head down. You'll make a good shift to your left side and square the face for straighter shots.

THE DECISION LINE

I make all my decisions behind the ball. Once I'm standing over the ball, my thinking is done. My club and body are set, and I swing without hesitation. But most amateurs do the opposite: They spend little time behind the ball and an eternity over it. They think about line, club selection, setup, and the lesson they had on the driving range last week. All this invites is indecision and fear, making it almost impossible to put a good swing on the ball.

Imagine a line several feet behind the ball (I've laid a shaft on the ground here to demonstrate). Call it your "decision" line. Once you cross this line, your brain is done thinking. You're committed to the club, the shot, and the target. If, for any reason, you're uncomfortable with any of the decisions you've made, step back and start again.

It's okay to have one swing thought when you're over the ball—"Take the club back low," perhaps, or "Make a good shoulder turn." But if you have more than one swing thought at decision time, you're hurting yourself when you're over the ball. You need to keep it simple: Just aim, set your body, and go. You'll be surprised how much more consistent you are off the tee if you take less time over the ball.

• •

Before I step up to the ball, I know exactly what type of shot I'm going to play and where I want to leave my approach. My intentions are clear. This way, when I step over the "decision line" (represented here by the shaft on the ground), there's no hesitation. I aim the clubface at my target, set my stance, and go, leaving no time for fear or indecision to creep in.

PRESHOT ROUTINE: MY COMFORT ZONE

While shooting 59 in the second round of the 2001 Standard Register Ping, I birdied the first eight holes and 12 of the first 13. So it was hard not to look ahead and calculate the possibilities in my head: *If I birdie this hole, I'm at 59. Birdie the next and that's 58*. But I knew if I let my mind wander, I'd be in trouble. I had to regain my focus—to play one shot at a time. Fortunately, I had a secret weapon: my preshot routine.

No matter how I'm playing, I go through the same routine before every tee shot. This keeps me comfortable and does wonders for my consistency. Here's the routine:

First, I consult my caddie about the distance and the type of shot I want to play, then I choose a club (*right*). Next, I walk directly behind the ball and pick out my target line. I take a few practice swings, visualizing the shot I want to hit, and then step back to finalize the line. When I'm ready, I walk up to the ball. Once I'm there, the first thing I do is aim the clubface perpendicular to the target line. I look for an intermediate target—a leaf, a twig, a brown spot on the grass—a foot or two in front of the ball

along the target line, because I find it's easier to aim at an object close to me than one that's 100 or more yards away.

I align my body and take one long, last look at the target, making sure my arms and shoulders are relaxed. Then I pull the trigger.

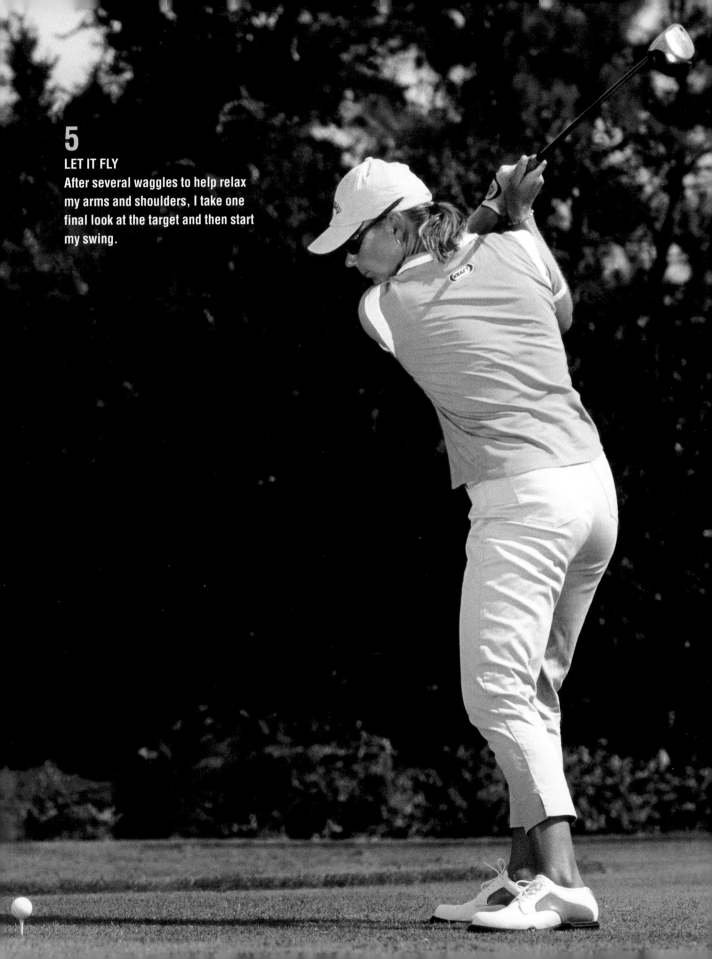

5

LET IT FLY

After several waggles to help relax my arms and shoulders, I take one final look at the target and then start my swing.

BRUSH THE GROUND

The typical amateur hits the ground with his driver as he makes a practice swing. Sometimes he even takes a divot. This promotes a steep swing and very often results in an embarrassing pop fly.

Remember—the ball is teed up in the air for your drive. To make solid contact, the head of your driver must be in the air, too. That's why a drive requires a much shallower angle of approach than an iron. When you take a practice swing, you should gently brush the top blades of grass with the bottom of your clubhead. You'll make a flatter swing and avoid those dreaded pop-ups.

WORKING THE BALL

That final tee shot at the 2003 Women's British Open set up perfectly for me. My natural shot is a slight draw, and I knew I wouldn't have any trouble clearing the bunkers on the right side of the fairway. I could aim at the right rough and bend the ball back toward the middle. No problem. And that's exactly what I did, splitting the fairway with a big blast of 285 yards.

But at the Colonial, I wasn't that lucky. The 470-yard par-4 fifth hole at Colonial Country Club, the last hole in Colonial's "Horrible Horseshoe," gave me fits. In the first round, I thought I'd hit a pretty straight drive, but my tee shot bounced left into a ditch. I made my first bogey of the tournament there.

In the second round, I tried to fade the ball so it wouldn't hit the same slope again. I set up for a left-to-right shot, but I blocked it well to the right into the trees. I had another bogey.

That fifth at Colonial might be the toughest hole I've ever played. Standing on the tee, I thought, "Where do I go? You can't be left here; you can't be right." Most holes give you a choice.

The ability to work the ball in either direction helps open up the fairway, making it easier to keep the ball in play.

On that final drive at the 2003 British Open, I could bail out to the right.

Almost every hole in golf favors either a right-to-left shot, or a left-to-right shot. Good golfers need to be able to play both. The ability to work the ball in either direction helps open up the fairway, making it easier to keep the ball in play. To become an expert player you must learn to make the ball curve left *or* right.

The clubhead should travel slightly on the upswing at impact, sweeping the ball off the tee (*right*). This requires a flatter angle of approach, which you can groove with your practice swing. Brush the ground with your rehearsal swing, hearing the "swoosh" of the clubhead as it travels through the air.

DRAW FOR DISTANCE

A draw is a shot that moves slightly from right to left (for right-handed golfers, that is). It's a controlled version of a hook. Due to the ball's right-to-left spin and lower trajectory, a draw tends to roll farther than a fade. So if you're trying to squeeze out a few extra yards, here's the shot for you.

Start by aiming the clubface directly at the

target. Close your stance by pointing your feet, hips, and shoulders right of the target—or where you want the ball to start flying. Now make your normal swing. Because the clubface is closed relative to the path of your swing, it will put a right-to-left spin on the ball.

It also helps to tee the ball high, so at least half the ball sits above the top of your driver. The higher you tee it, the flatter your swing.

With practice, you'll develop a sweeping action that promotes the in-to-out swing path you'll need to draw the ball.

· ·

Tee the ball slightly higher than normal for a draw. To hit the ball on the center of the clubface, you'll have to swing on a flatter, more in-to-out path.

FADE FOR CONTROL

A fade is a shot that moves slightly from left to right (for right-handed golfers)—a more controlled version of a slice. The ball tends to climb higher and land more softly with less roll than a draw.

To hit a fade, simply adjust your alignment from the draw. Again, aim the clubface first—perpendicular to the target—but this time, open your stance by pointing your feet, hips, and shoulders left of the

target line. Now swing along your body line again. Because the clubface is open relative to your swing path, the ball starts to the left and curves back to the right.

Teeing the ball lower, so that only a fraction of the ball is above your driver, can also help you hit a fade. The lower the ball, the more likely you are to hit down on it. Hitting down promotes an out-to-in path and a steep angle of approach, which tends to put left-to-right spin on the ball.

• •

Tee the ball slightly lower than normal to produce a fade. You'll be forced to steepen your angle of approach, which encourages a left-to-right ball.

ANNIKA'S KEYS TO DRIVING

During my rookie season on the LPGA Tour, I averaged just over 229 yards per drive. But in 2003 I led the tour with an average drive of 270—an increase of 41 yards! I'm reaching par-5s in two that I couldn't touch five years ago, and hitting less club into the greens than most other players. Along with the fact that I'm as accurate as ever, that's a huge advantage. How did I do it? With a lot of hard work in the gym and a smooth, effortless tempo I grooved over the years.

- Swing under control with the same tempo you would use for a wedge shot, maintaining your balance into the finish.
- On your backswing, pretend your body is turning inside an imaginary cylinder, rotating your right hip straight back.
- Start down slowly from the top, giving your hands, arms, and body a chance to move down together.
- As you swing through impact, allow your head to follow the ball, releasing it toward the target.
- Make all your swing and alignment decisions behind the ball, not when you're standing over it. If you change your mind while addressing the ball, back off and line up the shot again.

$\mathcal{A}$ccurate Irons

HOW TO HIT MORE GREENS

I'm a perfectionist. My goal is to hit every fairway, one-putt every green, and birdie every hole. It's my vision to shoot 54, and it wouldn't be possible without a pinpoint iron game. My greens-in-regulation stat has hovered around 80 percent (79.7 percent in 2001 and '02; although my GIR percentage dropped to 75.5 percent in 2003, it was still tops on Tour), which is a big reason I've won five Vare Trophies, given to the LPGA Tour player with the lowest scoring average.

When I won my first Nabisco Championship in 2001, I hit 35 of 36 greens on Saturday and Sunday. That's a performance I'll never forget. Mission Hills Country Club in Rancho Mirage, California, is a course that demands precision iron shots, and I was throwing darts that week. Accuracy is also essential at the Colonial on the PGA Tour. That's why I chose Colonial Country Club when I decided to test myself against the best male players in the world. Of all the venues I considered, Colonial put the biggest premium on accuracy. It was longer than any course I've ever played on the LPGA Tour, but it dictated that you place off the tee, not bomb it as far as you can. In many instances, I used the same club as the guys for my second shot. In fact, I was surprised at the number of short irons I played that week. Unfortunately, I can't spin the ball like the guys do—that takes brute strength—so I couldn't get as close to a lot of the pins as they could. Still, I had my fair share of birdie opportunities throughout the two days I played, and my iron play had a lot do with that.

Tiger Woods wrote that "the irons are the true offensive weapons in golf." I couldn't agree more. The more greens you hit, the more birdie chances you have. If you want to shoot lower scores, you have to hit solid iron shots.

THE FIRST RULE OF IRON PLAY: DOWN MAKES UP

Golf is a game of opposites. Think back to my chapter on driving: If you want to hit the ball farther, your instincts may tell you to swing harder, but what you really must do is swing smoothly. In iron play, you must hit down on the ball to make it go up. Yet the average golfer, seeing that the ball is on the ground and not teed up, tries to lift it into the air.

A descending blow makes the ball rebound off the clubface with a tremendous amount of backspin, or reverse spin, which makes the ball rise. The clubface contacts the bottom of the ball before reaching its low point in front of the ball—that's why a good player's divot is always on the target side of the ball. If the clubhead bottoms out too soon, which is usually the case when amateurs scoop the ball, the shot comes out either heavy or thin.

A descending blow is necessary to generate the backspin required to lift the ball into the air.

BALL POSITION: PUSH IT FORWARD

How do you ensure a descending blow? Start with ball position. As I discussed in Chapter 2, I play the ball about an inch forward of center in my stance with mid-irons, and between the center and my left heel with longer irons. Each position represents the low point of my swing, where the club should bottom out. If you're not sure where the low point is, take note of where your divots are on the range and adjust your ball position accordingly.

Why play the ball ahead of center for most irons? Because the longer the club, the more aggressively your body must rotate through the shot. This moves the swing's low point forward. The farther back the ball is, the less time you have to transfer your weight forward on the downswing, and the earlier the clubhead hits the ground. That's okay for the shorter clubs that don't require a big swing, but with a 5-iron, you need more time to release the club. Moving the ball forward in your stance gives you the precious split second you need for solid impact.

• •

I play the ball about an inch forward of center in my stance for a mid-iron (*left*), and between my sternum and left heel for a longer iron. This gives me more time to release the club. Take several practice swings with each club to see where the low point of your swing is (i.e., the center of your divot), and position the ball there.

I try to keep my right arm fairly straight in the back-swing (*left*), which encourages me to turn—rather than lift—my shoulders to the top (*above*). My left shoulder rotates directly under my chin.

BACKSWING: TURN, DON'T LIFT

I take the club back slowly. My right shoulder leads the way, almost as if it were pulling my hands, arms, shoulders, and hips along. This starts the club on the correct path, slightly inside the target line. As my shoulders turn, the club moves farther up and in. There's no need to lift the club.

When I get in trouble, it's because I forget that important fact—my tempo quickens and I dip the left shoulder. Then, up comes my right shoulder and I wind up lifting the club rather than turning my shoulders to the top. To ensure that I make a better turn, I try to keep my right arm as straight as possible on the backswing. This forces me to turn the shoulders to the top and promotes a wider arc.

In a good backswing turn, my left shoulder rotates past the ball, directly under my chin. It almost covers my chin. To get a sense of how this move should feel, have someone give your shoulder a nudge, as if you were pushing through a turnstile (my coach, Henri Reis, demonstrates below). As I continue my backswing, I feel the muscles behind my left shoulder stretching. That's good—it means I've established a nice, tight coil. I'm in the perfect position to swing down and send the ball on its way.

DOWNSWING: START AT THE BOTTOM

I initiate the downswing by pushing my right foot and knee forward. This bump from the lower body shifts my weight to my front side, setting the rest of my downswing in motion. My arms start down, then my hips and shoulders turn out of the way, making room for my right side to "fire through" the ball.

As my right leg moves forward, my left knee turns outward, almost as if it's forming a reverse C. The bend in my left knee shows that my legs are driving forward toward the target.

Too many amateurs start the downswing

with their hands. That pulls the right shoulder out, throwing the club over the top on a steep out-to-in path. The result is a weak, arms-only swing. By initiating the downswing with your lower body—from the ground up—you'll keep the club on an inside-out path. Do that and you'll soon be hitting straighter, more consistent shots.

I initiate the downswing by driving my right knee and foot toward the target (*opposite page*). This shifts my weight forward, allowing the rest of the downswing to work in the proper sequence. The arms start down first (*below*), then my hips and shoulders turn out of the way, clearing a path for my arms to swing.

DOWNSWING DRILLS

STEP AHEAD

To help my weight shift in the downswing, I often practice the "Step-Through Drill." Using a mid-iron, I make a normal swing but just before contact I stride toward the target with my right foot. As I step my weight moves to my front foot. The low point of the swing shifts forward, too, and the clubhead strikes the ball and then the ground, as it should.

RIGHT HAND ONLY

Another way to groove your downswing is to take practice swings with one hand. Grasp the front of your shirt with your left hand and swing away with your right hand only. You'll find that to make solid contact—and maintain your balance—you have to keep your hips and shoulders back just long enough to let your right arm catch up (*left*). Then your right side can release and fire through (*right*), making perfect contact.

So try to delay your hips and shoulders as you start down from the top. Let your right elbow drop almost into your right hip pocket, and you'll keep the club on the proper inside-out path to the ball.

IMPACT! MORE POWER TO YOU

On the practice range, I like to simulate impact conditions by making swings into a special beanbag called an impact bag. By using this training aid, I get a better idea of where the club and my body—particularly my hips, left arm, and left leg—are at impact. That's important information, because impact is the moment in the swing that matters most.

At impact, most of my weight is on my front foot, my hips are open, and my head is releasing to the target. My left leg is braced for the hit, and my left arm and the club's shaft are in a nearly straight line. I say nearly straight because the shaft is actually leaning slightly forward, toward the target. The club is still moving downward, accelerating forward and applying maximum force. The operative word is *downward*—even at impact, the club is still going down.

Again, you must not try to lift the ball. If you do, your wrists will unhinge early and the clubhead will lose speed, ensuring a weak strike.

That's why the sequencing of the downswing is so crucial. If your arms and body stay connected, you create room for your arms to swing down freely, while saving the split second you need to "sling" the clubhead into the ball. With everything in sync, your wrists stay hinged—or slightly bent—well into the downswing, straightening just after impact. This slinging action through the ball creates more clubhead speed—and more power as you connect.

• •

At impact, my weight is on my front foot (*opposite page*) and my left arm and clubshaft are in a relatively straight line. My right wrist remains slightly bent, creating an additional burst of speed as it straightens out through impact. The longer you're able to preserve the hinge in your wrists (*left*), the more power you can unleash through the ball.

THROUGH IMPACT: DON'T GET HIPPY

I'm constantly fighting my hips. They're too aggressive. In an attempt to generate more power, I sometimes let my hips slide forward on the downswing. Wrong! That move messes up the rest of my swing. My right shoulder drops, my weight stays back. From this position, I can't rotate my head and shoulders properly. I have to rely on my hands to square the clubface at the last second, and that's impossible to do consistently.

When I'm swinging well, the ball just gets in the way of my swing. At impact, my hips and shoulders have cleared, freeing up space for my right side to release through. Rather than sliding with my hips, I have turned them to make room for my right side to fire down and through the ball. That's where I get my power—from the right side. Not from the first move of my downswing, but from the last.

On the follow-through the clubhead moves almost straight ahead and my belly button points at the target (*right*). All my energy is directed at the target. I have accelerated the club through impact, making sure that the clubhead reaches the ball at maximum speed.

SHAKE HANDS IN THE FOLLOW-THROUGH

To train your right side to fire through properly, take your normal address posture and hold a club in your left hand. Extend your left arm toward the target so that the shaft is parallel to the ground and the clubhead points straight up. Now, reach over with your right hand as if you were going to shake hands with your left. You'll get a feel for shifting your weight forward. You can't join hands if your weight stays back.

As I reach to "shake hands," notice how my right shoulder turns down and through. That's key: The shoulders should rotate fairly level through impact.

Also, note the position of my club and body in the shake-hands position. This is where I want to be halfway into my follow-through. The clubhead is toe-up, an indication that I've released the club properly, and my hips and shoulders point left of the target—a sure sign that my right side has fired through correctly.

HOW I HIT MY LASER-LIKE 6-IRON

For two weeks in March 2001, I was in "the zone." Every green looked like a football field and my irons were throwing darts. At the Standard Register PING, I fired a 59 and made a career-high 29 birdies, hitting 92 percent (66 of 72) of the greens in regulation. I cooled off a little the following week at the Nabisco Championship, finding 62 of 72 greens, but for the two-week period I hit 128 of 144 greens, or 89 percent!

Of course, it helps that I was in the fairway most of the time and could hit a lot of short irons onto the greens. But the fundamentals for hitting a 4-iron are the same as they are for an 8-iron. It starts with a good setup, my arms hanging directly below my shoulders and my upper body tilted away

from the target. My butt is pushed out, giving my upper back a straight—not rounded—appearance. As I swing back, I try to keep my right arm as straight as possible. This forces me to turn my shoulders to the top, rather than lift them on too steep a plane. My left shoulder rotates past the ball, directly under my chin, creating a tight, strong coil and storing momentum for the downswing.

I initiate the downswing with my lower body, transferring my weight to my front foot before starting down with my hands and arms. My hips and shoulders stay back just long enough for my right arm to catch up. As long as my arms and body maintain this connection, my right side will release and fire through, consistently squaring the clubface.

When hitting a 3- or 4-iron, make the same *easy* swing as you would with your 8-iron.

LONG IRONS: NICE AND EASY

At the Colonial, I was on equal footing with most of the men when I had a short iron in my hands. But when the distance stretched to 180 or 190 yards, I was at a big disadvantage. I hit some pretty good iron shots that week. During the first round, I flushed a couple of 6-irons—one stopped only 15 feet from the cup on No. 13 to set up my first PGA Tour birdie, and another, from 171 yards on No. 15, was almost as close to the pin. On 18,

I hit a big 4-iron from 192 yards to 30 feet.

Earlier in my career, I struggled with my long irons. It got so bad that at one point the 5-iron was the longest iron I carried in my bag, and I relied heavily on my fairway woods. But today, thanks to my increased strength, I'm able to swing these clubs with confidence. Now, I can

A 3- or 4-iron doesn't look very forgiving, and the lack of loft makes them difficult to hit. But the last thing you want to do with these clubs is try to help the ball up— or even worse—swing hard. Think nice and easy.

generate more clubhead speed with a swing that's as smooth and easy as the one I use with my pitching wedge. And that's the key to hitting longer irons. It's taken me years to realize it, but you don't have to swing harder to hit the ball farther.

That's what I'm always telling my pro-am playing partners today. A 3- or 4-iron doesn't look very forgiving, and the lack of loft makes them difficult to hit. But the last thing you want to do

with these clubs is try to help the ball up—or even worse—swing hard. Think *nice and easy*. The next time you're hitting a 4-iron, make the same swing as you would with your 8-iron. You'll stay balanced, and your arms and body will have a better chance of staying connected. You'll make solid contact, which is the first step toward shooting better scores.

ANNIKA'S KEYS TO IRON PLAY

One reason I decided to play at Colonial was that the course puts a premium on iron play. Length off the tee isn't as big a necessity there; the most important thing is to position the ball in the middle of the fairway and hit it close to the flag. And that's my biggest strength: I hit a lot of greens, which requires a solid all-around iron game.

- Hit down on the ball to make it go up, leaving a divot on the target side of the ball.
- On the backswing, rotate your left shoulder past the ball until it is directly below your chin.
- Start the downswing with your lower body, shifting your weight to your front side before starting down with your hands and arms.
- Maintain the hinge in your wrists well into the downswing, slinging the clubhead through the ball.

5 Fairway Woods

A LOFTY ALTERNATIVE

When I teed it up in the first round of the 1996 U.S. Women's Open at Pine Needles, I had five woods in my bag—1, 3, 5, 7, and 9. I substituted the 9-wood for my 4-iron. The 7-wood replaced my 3-iron. Why so many woods? Because the greens at Pine Needles are firm, and that forces players to hit high, soft approach shots. That's easier to do with a 9-wood than with a 4-iron. At the time, I also found the woods to be easier to hit than long irons, so the choice was a no-brainer.

Today, I carry only three woods in my bag—driver, 4, and 7. There are two reasons for this: first, as I mentioned last chapter, I'm striking my long irons much better these days; and second, using fewer woods allows me to carry more wedges.

The upshot is that my 4- and 7-woods still get a pretty healthy workout. On the LPGA Tour, I'll hit at least one 7-wood per round (at the '96 Open, I hit about five per round), and that's only counting shots from the fairway. Off the tee, it's another story. At Colonial, my club of choice on the much-anticipated first tee shot was a 4-wood. I hit a 4-wood off the tee four more times that day and 7-wood once. It was the same during the second round.

I don't lose much yardage with the 4-wood. Off the tee, I carry it about 225 yards; off the deck, about 215. Depending on the amount of roll I get, that usually means about 25 to 30 yards fewer than with my driver. If you're an amateur golfer, you may not realize how little yardage difference there is between your driver and 3-wood. You should probably hit 3-, 4-, or 7-wood off the tee more often. The 3-wood is shorter and easier to control than the driver. It also has more loft, so you can get the ball airborne more easily. Many amateurs hit their 3-woods just as far as they hit their drivers—and some hit them even farther. So play smarter! Take the shorter club and keep it in the short grass.

MY LUCKY SEVEN

The 7-wood is one of my favorite clubs, for several reasons. First of all, I love the way it sits behind the ball (*right*). It looks super-easy to hit because it has so much loft. Also, the 7 is a little shorter than the other woods I carry, so it's easier to control. Finally, it's quite effective from the rough—much better than a long iron. There's more mass behind the face, which allows the club to cut through the grass. The clubhead

HOW I HIT MY 7-WOOD STRAIGHT AND TRUE

Entering the final round of the 2001 Tyco/ADT Tour Championship at Trump International Golf Club in West Palm Beach, Florida, I needed to shoot a 5-under 65 to set a new LPGA single-season scoring record. (At least that's what I thought I had to shoot—it turned out a 66 would have gotten the job done!) I fired a 65, breaking the record by .01 strokes (69.42). And I did it by going 5-under on the back nine at Trump International. Given the blustery conditions and difficulty of the course (Karrie Webb and I were the only players under par that week), it was pretty much a miracle.

The key shot of my back-nine blitz was a 7-wood that settled 12 feet from the pin on the par-5 15th hole. I slam-dunked my eagle putt to move to 4-under on the day, and completed my 65 with a birdie on the par-3 17th.

doesn't twist as much on its way through the rough, and that means straighter shots.

I've hit a lot of big 7-wood shots over the years, probably none better than the approach I made on the 3rd hole during Round 1 of the Colonial. The long, dogleg-left par-4, the first in the difficult three-hole "Horrible Horseshoe" stretch, requires a well-placed tee shot around the corner of the dogleg, and then a long approach. At 476 yards, it's a monster of a hole. After a perfect drive, I had 213 yards to the pin and hit as pure a 7-wood as I could ever imagine—13 feet from the hole.

Most golfers should carry at least three woods. If you really struggle with your long irons, you may want to add a fourth. The 7-wood is a great choice. I carry mine about 195 yards (205 off the tee), which is about 3-iron distance. If the choice is between a long iron and a lofted wood, amateurs should always opt for the simpler, smarter play: Hit a fairway wood.

Another 7-wood approach shot had set up my 13th and final birdie in a round of 59 earlier that year in Phoenix.

To make the 7-wood *your* lucky club, let its loft do the work. Place the ball forward of center in your stance, keeping the shaft almost vertical and your hands directly below your chin. As you swing back, try to maintain the triangle formed by your arms and shoulders, making sure to complete your turn so your back points to the target at the top. On the way down, think "smooth and easy" as your body unwinds toward the target. The club should approach the ball on a very shallow path—almost level to the ground—sweeping the ball into the air on a nice, high trajectory.

ADDRESS: SET UP TO SWEEP IT

The fairway woods are designed to sweep the ball off the turf, generating distance with additional lofts and longer shafts. You don't have to hit down on the ball as much as you would with an iron—instead, you make more of a U-shaped swing. The clubhead brushes along the ground, launching the ball into the air.

To make a flatter approach, you need to adjust your setup. First, play the ball ahead of center in your stance, as you would with a long iron—between the middle of your

Tempo is critical, so keep your arms and shoulders relaxed.

stance and your left heel. Start with the shaft nearly vertical, or straight up and down—not angled forward or back—to take advantage of the club's full loft. Tempo is critical, so keep your arms and shoulders relaxed. Your hands should hang directly under your chin. This puts you the proper distance from the ball and promotes a wide, circular-shaped swing arc. Your arms shouldn't reach toward the ball as you set up; they must be relaxed.

At address, the shaft is nearly vertical (*left*) and my hands are directly under my chin (*right*), which promotes a wide, sweeping shape to my swing.

BACKSWING: TRIANGLE TO THE TOP

As I start my backswing, I concentrate on keeping my hands, arms, and shoulders moving together—maintaining the triangle formed by my arms and shoulders at address. This one-piece action sets a smooth pace and promotes a wide, sweeping shape to the swing. It also helps start the club on the correct path.

The first foot or so of my swing should resemble the last few inches before impact, with the clubhead sweeping along the ground. I try not to lift the club too quickly, pulling it back with my shoulders, arms, and hands. As the clubhead reaches waist-height, I feel as if my chest is over my right leg. The shaft should now be parallel to the target line, with my wrists slightly hinged. From this point on, I simply focus on finishing my turn.

At the top, I've turned my back to the target. From this fully coiled position, my body starts down toward the ball, calmly accelerating the clubhead into impact.

• •

As I swing back, I try to maintain the triangle formed by my arms and shoulders at address (*left*). My back faces the target at the top of the swing (*below*).

At Colonial, I hit 4-wood as frequently as I hit driver, using it to split the fairway with my opening drive on the par-4 10th hole.

BRUSH A SECOND BALL AWAY

Many golfers snatch the club to the inside on the takeaway, causing them to lift their arms to the top. This narrows the swing's arc, setting up a steep, out-to-in downswing path—the recipe for a slice.

To swing with a wider arc and less lifting, set up to address a ball as you normally would, then put a second ball down directly behind the first, just outside your back foot. Swing the club back slowly, rolling the second ball gently out of the way with the back of the clubhead. If you pick the club up too soon, you'll have a hard time touching—let alone rolling—the second ball.

I use this drill to fix the bad habit of dipping my left shoulder in the backswing, which creates too much lift. Using two balls ensures that I keep my shoulders level. I feel as if I'm moving the clubhead straight back—the right start for the sweeping, U-shaped swing I want with my fairway woods.

LET YOUR SWING FLOW

Want a great way to smooth your takeaway and encourage a wide, sweeping arc? Try making practice swings by starting from a post-impact position. Extend the clubhead about three feet in front of your normal ball position and swing back in a single, flowing motion. Feel how smooth and easy that is? Try making several practice swings this way, then take it to the next step: Start in the post-impact position and hit a few balls for real. Next time you're on the course, try to swing with the same free-flowing motion.

If you're like a lot of amateurs, you have trouble pulling the trigger on your swing. You sometimes jerk the club back, picking it up on the takeaway instead of dragging it back smoothly and slowly. This drill can smooth out those initial bumps, relaxing tight muscles and promoting a wide arc.

IMPACT: MAKE A CLEAN SWEEP

A shallow approach to the ball helps me pick the ball cleanly off the grass with my fairway woods. I may ruffle a few blades of grass on impact, but there's no divot. Once my swing starts, all I think about is making a complete turn—getting my back to point at the target—maintaining a smooth rhythm and balance. I don't want to swing hard or hit down on the ball, I simply unwind my body and let the club's loft do the rest. That's a great thought for amateurs: Don't think about hitting the ball; just let it get in the way of your swing.

A shallow approach allows me to sweep the ball off the ground, utilizing the club's full loft to get the ball airborne (*opposite page*). My swing remains balanced into the finish (*left*).

NO FEAR

Fairway woods are sometimes called "utility woods," and with good reason. They are very versatile clubs that are easy to hit and are capable of handling just about any lie—rough, sand, sidehill. Yet many amateurs won't hit a fairway wood from a poor lie, even if it's the only way to reach the green.

They reach for the less-lofted 4- or 5-irons, figuring it's better to be short than sideways.

That's no way to help your scores, and there's no reason to fear hitting a fairway wood from an uphill, downhill, or sidehill lie, if you make the proper adjustments. Here's how:

· ·

(*Right*): On an uphill lie, align your hips and shoulders parallel to the slope. Do the same for a downhill lie, moving the ball slightly farther back in your stance (*far right*) and swinging with the slope.

UNEVEN LIES: SWING WITH THE SLOPE

For a shot from any uneven lie, the secret is to align your shoulders with the slope beneath the ball. From an uphill lie, I set up with my shoulders and hips parallel to the rising slope, which helps me swing along the slope rather than down into it. I play the ball forward in my stance, and use a less-lofted club—a 3- or 4-wood instead of a 5- or 7-wood—letting the hill help me launch the ball into the air. I will aim to the right of the target, since the shot will tend to fly high and left, and finish with my weight forward, over my front leg. I also make sure to finish my swing—too many amateurs hit and fall back from an uphill shot.

For a downhill lie, I still want to set up with my hips and shoulders parallel to the slope. I will play the ball an inch farther back than I would on a level lie. The down-slope will make the ball fly lower and roll more, so I go with a more-lofted club—a 5-wood instead of a 3-wood, for instance. The ball will tend to fly right, so I aim to the left of the target.

SIDEHILL LIES: SIT DOWN OR SIT UP

When the ball is below my feet, my main concern is keeping my balance. To reach the ball, I bend more than usual from my knees and hips, getting into a lower, "sitting" position. I play the ball farther back in my stance, as I would with a downhill lie, and aim farther left because the ball will tend to curve to the right. I keep my legs steady (and position more weight toward my heels) and make an arms-and-upper-body swing. I don't want much leg movement—in this swing, balance is what counts.

When the ball is above my feet, it is closer to my hands. Now I must stand taller and grip down several inches to maintain the proper distance to

• •

(*Left*): When the ball is above your feet, grip down to maintain the correct distance to the ball. (*Inset*): When the ball is below your feet, bend more at the knees to get down to the ball.

the ball. Most golfers hit this shot fat—they either forget to change their grip or they stand too far from the ball and top it. But if you set up properly, gripping down and aiming to the right—this shot tends to curve left—you can make this tricky sidehill shot look easy.

I had just such a lie on the 72nd hole of regulation at the 2003 McDonald's LPGA Championship at DuPont Country Club in Wilmington, Delaware. Needing a par to force a playoff with Grace Park, my tee shot (a 4-wood) landed in the first cut of rough, about 200 yards from the flag. The ball was slightly above my feet, so I gripped down on my 7-wood about an inch and let it rip. The ball carried the right greenside bunker and landed safely on the green, about pin high and 25 feet from the hole. From there, I two-putted and forced a playoff, which I won on the same par-4 18th hole. Considering how much trouble that hole was giving me up to that point, it was nice to exact some revenge on it.

ANNIKA'S KEYS TO FAIRWAY WOODS

At one point in my career, I carried five woods in my bag. Today I'm down to three. But to underscore the importance of these clubs, consider the one club I chose for the biggest shot of my life—the opening tee shot at the Colonial. It was a 4-wood. I love these clubs. Off the tee, they're much easier to control than a driver. And on approach shots, they produce a higher trajectory and a softer landing than their iron counterparts, a big plus when you're chasing birdies and the occasional eagle.

- Start with the shaft nearly vertical at address, and position your hands under your chin to promote a wider, more circular swing arc.
- The first 18 inches of your swing should resemble the last few inches prior to impact, with the clubhead sweeping along the ground.
- Don't think about *hitting* the ball; just let it get in the way of your swing.
- Make more of a "U"-shaped swing versus a "V"; do not take a divot.
- From uneven lies, align your hips and shoulders parallel to the slope.

Wedge Play

HOW TO KNOCK IT STIFF

With a wedge in my hands, I expect to get the ball down in two—whatever the distance. So you could imagine my surprise when I airmailed the 9th green with my 54-degree wedge during the final round of the 2004 McDonald's LPGA Championship. The poor approach led to a rare double bogey, and what had been a comfortable seven-shot lead was suddenly down to four.

My lead was just two shots when I reached the tee at the par-5 16th hole at DuPont Country Club. Again, my 54-degree wedge would play a crucial role in deciding the championship. After pulling my tee shot into the rough on the adjacent 11th hole, I decided to play down the 11th fairway instead of punching out sideways. I wound up 94 yards from the pin—a perfect distance for my sand wedge—but I had a mountain of trees to climb to get there.

Had my lead been five or six shots, I would have probably played my third shot a little left of the flag, where the branches weren't so high. But I wanted to win, so I decided to take the high road and fire directly at the flag. Terry, my caddie, said to me, "Just pretend I'm standing by the pin with my mitt"—a favorite drill I use to sharpen my distance control (*left*). I opened the clubface a little bit and swung hard but under control. The ball high-jumped the trees and landed on the green, spinning back to three feet to set up an easy birdie. My lead was three shots again and now there was nothing stopping me from winning my seventh major, and second of back-to-back McDonald's titles.

Under the circumstances, it was one of the best shots of my career. I mean, it took some guts; the trees were at least 60 feet high. But I've practiced that shot so many times before—granted, with no trees—that I can hit it in my sleep. One bad shot is not going to take my confidence away.

FOUR WEDGES, ONE SWING

Almost seven years ago, on the advice of my former caddie, Colin Cann, I retired my 5-wood and added a fourth wedge to my bag. This wasn't long after I had won my second U.S. Women's Open championship in 1996. At the time, I was hitting 5-wood maybe twice a tournament, whereas I might hit a wedge five or six times per round. It just made sense to switch.

With four wedges, I have a club for almost every yardage. Under normal conditions, a full swing with my 58-degree lob wedge carries 80 yards; my 54-degree wedge produces a 95-yard shot; my 48-degree wedge flies 105 yards; and my pitching wedge goes 115. My favorite distance to the flag is 80 yards, so if I have to lay up, I'll try to leave my ball 80 yards from the pin. If there's trouble there, I'll lay up to 95 or 115 yards. By using different wedges, I can put the same swing on the ball and be precise from various distances. This repeating action helps me stick my short approaches close—usually within six to fifteen feet of the hole.

If you carry only one or two wedges, as many amateurs do, then you're constantly changing the length and pace of your swing to vary distance. If you hit your pitching wedge 110 yards, you have to make a shorter swing to hit it 95 yards. That's when golf becomes guesswork (*how far back do I swing?*). You're better off carrying the right tools for the task.

• •

Carrying four wedges allows me to cover a lot of ground using the same repeating swing (*right*).

DISTANCE CONTROL DRILL

PLAY BALL!

No matter how many wedges you carry, you should know approximately how far you hit each with a full swing, a three-quarter swing, and a half swing.

A good way to find out is to build your own mini driving range. Place a cone, headcover, or other object every 10 yards, and try and land balls on these targets, changing the length of your swing to suit the shot. I do this all the time—even out on Tour when I'm by myself. But if either my husband or caddie is around, I'll have them grab a baseball glove and I'll hit balls to them. Starting at 80 yards with a full lob wedge, I proceed in 15-yard increments up to 110 yards—just short of a full pitching wedge. Sometimes, I'll even hit 7-, 8-, and 9-irons this way. The object is to hit balls so close to my centerfielder that he can catch them without taking a step (*right*). If I can do that, I know I can knock it stiff on the course.

I love this drill because it gives me a precise target and a precise distance. Having a body out there helps me focus on a specific target without the usual distractions—bunkers, water, trees. The narrower your focus, the easier it is to hit your target.

DIALING IN THE PERFECT DISTANCE

While practicing for the Colonial, I took the "Play Ball!" drill a step further and had my caddie radio each shot's distance back to me via walkie-talkie. I wanted to build more precision with my short irons and wedges, and the instant feedback that Terry McNamara gave me helped tremendously. If I wanted to take a little off my pitching wedge and hit the ball 110 yards, I knew within seconds if I'd pulled off the shot. With repetition, I improved my distance control. Using walkie-talkies may sound a little extreme, but think about it: On Tour, two or three yards can easily be the difference between knocking it close and missing the green entirely.

• • • • • • • • • • • • • • • • • • •

To build more precision into my wedge game, I started using a walkie-talkie on the range.

SETUP: NARROW YOUR STANCE

Wedge play is all about control, not power. That's why the setup is narrower with a wedge than with a driver. I set my feet about shoulder-width apart, never wider, distributing my weight evenly over both feet. This narrow stance promotes a short, compact swing—a key to control— and helps to quiet my legs so I can use more of my arms and body throughout the swing. The narrower your stance, the easier it is to rotate your body through the shot.

I take a slightly open stance, as if I were playing a fade. That creates space for my arms to swing down freely. The ball is opposite my sternum, in the middle of my stance. This promotes a steeper angle of approach to the ball: The clubhead bottoms out just in front of my sternum, launching the ball high with plenty of backspin.

A narrow stance encourages more of an arms-and-body swing, which leads to greater control. My stance is slightly open, creating room for my arms to swing down freely.

PARTIAL SHOTS: TURN BACK THE CLOCK

If I can't reach the green, I lay up to full-wedge distance—that comfort zone 80 to 115 yards from the green—because it's harder to make a three-quarter or half-swing from 50, 60, or 70 yards. It's much easier to repeat your swing and stay in rhythm with a full backswing.

Unfortunately, most amateurs are unwilling to lay up. They knock their approach shots as close to the green as possible, even if they can't get home. As a result, they face a lot of testy partial shots into the green.

You should play smarter than that—lay up to full-wedge distance!

Still, there are tactics that can help you improve on partial-wedge shots. Here's one of the best: To regulate the length of my backswing,

I pretend I'm standing in the center of a clockface with my head at 12 o'clock and my feet at 6. To hit the ball a shorter distance, similar to a half wedge, I swing my left arm back to 9 o'clock. For a slightly longer shot, to 10 o'clock, and, for a full shot, to 11 o'clock. The longer the shot, the closer my left arm gets to 11.

But, here's the key: I always follow through at least as far as I went back. If my arms swing back to 10 o'clock, they finish at 2 o'clock or beyond. I usually follow through a bit farther than I swing back, which helps me maintain a steady rhythm throughout the swing.

I like using the mental image of the clock because it takes a lot of uncertainty out of the backswing: It's easier to relate your arms to the numbers on a clock face. Even more important is accelerating the clubhead through impact.

Most golfers struggle with partial shots because they either fail to take the club back far enough and then hurry the downswing, or they swing back too far and decelerate at impact. If you swing the clubhead back and through the same amount, you can make crisp contact every time.

KILLING 'EM SOFTLY

The ball spins more coming off a wedge than any other club. It flies higher, lands softer—and if there's enough spin on it—rolls backward when it bites the green. The fans love to see the ball being spun back as if it were pulled on a string. This takes clubhead speed, clean grooves on the face of your club, and a razor-sharp angle of attack to make the ball dance.

The shot I play is determined by pin location. If the pin is up front, I may shoot for the center of the green and spin the ball backward. If the pin is back, I may play a lower shot, with less spin, so that the ball lands short of the flag and rolls toward it. But nine out of ten times, I hit a simpler shot: I let the club's true loft do the work, stopping the ball quickly without making it hop and back up.

As I swing, I try to keep my right palm pointing at the target through impact—almost as if I'm hitting a cut shot. This keeps the right hand from turning over too soon. The clubface might be slightly open at impact, but that's okay—it makes for an even softer landing.

• •

At impact, my right palm points at the target (*left*). This prevents the right hand from turning over too soon, leaving the clubface slightly open and producing a high, soft-landing shot.

I swing the club back with my arms and shoulders, turning my back to the target.

BASIC WEDGE SWING

My tempo for full and partial wedge shots is the same as it is for a 5-iron, but because the swing is shorter, it is slower-paced and not as powerful. As I swing back, I keep my right foot planted as long as I can. I focus on turning my chest over my right knee so that my back faces the target. As you work on this shot, be sure to move the club back with your arms and shoulders. Too many amateurs pick the club straight up with their hands, which limits the turn they can make when they swing.

If I'm turning properly, the butt end of my club will point to a spot just behind the ball—on the target line—when my arms are parallel to the ground.

On the downswing, I keep my arms and torso moving together through impact. There's very little wrist or lower-body action. My power comes from the length of the backswing and the speed of my body's forward rotation. My key thought is: Rotate my chest so it faces the target!

• • • • • • • • • • • • • • •

I rotate my arms and body through together so my chest faces the target at the completion of the swing.

MAKE A CONNECTION

To get a feel for how your arms and body should work together, put a headcover under your left arm and make half-, three-quarter, and full swings with a wedge. If your arms and body get out of sync with each other, the headcover will fall. But if you keep your arms, club, and chest moving together, it will stay in place.

This drill can help you to stop "scooping"—a common fault among amateurs. When you scoop the ball, you fail to rotate through to the target; instead, your body stalls at impact. The club keeps going, causing the left wrist to break down and the clubhead to bottom out behind the ball. But if you keep your body moving, the shaft will line up with your front arm at impact, the way it should.

FEET TOGETHER

One of the best drills of all—not just for wedge play, but for your entire game—is swinging with your feet together. It promotes good balance and tempo, and that's not all: It also trains you to use your lower body less, putting more emphasis on your arm swing and upper body rotation. The more you rotate your chest through the ball, the less you need to rely on your hands and wrists.

Your lower body does move with a wedge shot, but there's no need to create any extra power with your legs and hips. As long as your arms and chest accelerate through to the finish, you'll get all the power you need.

HOW I HIT MY WEDGES WITH PRECISION

Today, I can reach most par-5s in two shots. But if I can't, I still feel confident I can make birdie. That's because I possess a very accurate wedge game. Inside of 115 yards, I expect to get the ball up and down almost every time. With the amount of loft on each club, it's easier to control the distance than it is with, say, a 5-iron. I can hit a high-trajectory ball and stop it quickly, making it easier to get at the most difficult pin locations.

In the two sequences below, I'm hitting a full pitching wedge. That's key. I carry four wedges in my bag, so I'm able to cover a variety of different distances with the same full swing—from 80 to

115 yards. It's just a matter of repeating the same motion again and again.

Since wedge play is more about control than power, I set up with my feet closer together than normal, pointing slightly left of the target. This narrow, open stance helps quiet my lower body, encouraging more arm and body rotation through impact. On the downswing, I rotate my chest forward until it faces the target, making sure my follow-through is at least as long as my backswing. If I need to hit the ball farther, I speed up my body's rotation. The wedge swing is very much a body swing, which is why it's much easier to repeat. Instead of trying to time the release with my hands and wrists, my body rotation squares the face. The loft of the club does the rest.

LOW SHOT, LOW SPIN

Although I almost always lay up to full-wedge distance, the exceptions can make the game more challenging and more fun. If I'm hitting into a headwind or crosswind, that can alter my approach shot more than 10 yards, so I lay up as close to the green as possible and play a low shot in. I don't want to hit a full sand or lob wedge because the ball might get caught up in the wind and go off-target.

When playing into the wind, as I did on that final hole at the 2003 Weetabix Women's British Open, I take one of the lesser-lofted wedges in my bag, move the ball back in my stance, and make a three-quarter-length backswing. This imparts less backspin on the ball, creating a lower trajectory that penetrates the wind. To hit this delicate shot, you must resist the urge to swing hard, because the more clubhead speed you generate, the more backspin you'll produce and the higher the ball will climb.

At Royal Lytham & St. Annes, when I was tied for the lead at 10-under par with Se Ri Pak, I had only 109 yards to the flag after a 285-yard drive. Se Ri had to punch out after hitting her drive into a deep fairway bunker, so I had the upper hand and I wasn't about to do anything foolish to lose it. I just wanted to land the ball safely on the green and, if possible, give myself a decent run at birdie. I chose a line left of the flag and played a lower shot than

When playing into the wind…I take one of the lesser-lofted wedges in my bag, move the ball back in my stance, and make a three-quarter-length backswing. This imparts less backspin on the ball, creating a lower trajectory that penetrates the wind.

usual with less spin. The ball released a few feet and came to rest pin high, 12 feet left of the flag. I couldn't have hit a better shot under the circumstances. Two putts later—after Se Ri made bogey—I had my first British Open title, sixth major championship, and the career Grand Slam.

HIGH SHOT, HIGH FINISH

If the pin is tucked in front of a green and I need to bring the ball in high—so that it won't roll—I inch the ball slightly forward in my stance. My hands are now even with the clubhead, not ahead of it. Then I simply concentrate on swinging into a full finish position. I want the fat sole on the back of the wedge—called "the bounce" —to touch down first, just as it would on a greenside bunker shot.

To hit it high, play the ball slightly forward in your stance so that your hands are even with the club-head, and swing into a high finish position.

ANNIKA'S KEYS TO WEDGE PLAY

If I have a favorite distance for an approach shot, it's 80 yards. From there I feel like I can get it up and down every time. My wedge swing is almost all upper-body rotation, which is why it's so easy to repeat. I don't have to swing any harder to hit it farther; I just change lofts.

- Carry four wedges so you don't have to change the length of your swing to adjust to different distances.
- Narrow your stance—your feet should be shoulder-width apart— to promote more body rotation through the shot.
- Adjust the length of your backswing to vary the distance on your shots, always making sure to follow through the same amount as you swing back.
- Keep your arms and upper body moving together through impact, rotating your chest through until it faces the target.

The Short

Game

TURN 3 INTO 2 • BUNKER PLAY • PUTTING

7 Turn 3 into 2

CHIP AND PITCH IT CLOSE

For me, golf is all about taking my game to the next level. That's why I played in the Colonial, to test myself against the very best players in the world and learn a thing or two from them in the process. Seeing how the guys practiced, how they played certain shots around the green, how brilliantly they approached the game—I felt like a wide-eyed kid.

What I learned most that week reinforced what I already knew—that my short game needed big improvement. That's why the PGA Tour guys are so good. Sure, you always hear about Tiger Woods's length off the tee, or what driver he's playing, but it's his short game I admire most. And it's the same with most of the guys—they have the strength and the imagination to get it up and down from anywhere. The ball could be sitting down in the rough 10 paces from the hole, with the green running away from them, and they *expect* to get it close.

In the weeks leading up to the Colonial, I spent about 70 percent of my practice time on the short game, trying to improve my feel and confidence around the greens. And while it had no immediate impact on my performance at the Colonial, I did win my next two LPGA events, mostly due to the strength of my play around the greens. At the McDonald's LPGA Championship, just two weeks after the Colonial, I got up and down four times over the last eight holes on Sunday, including a marvelous 40-yard chip to three feet on the 14th hole. Almost two months later, I chipped in for a birdie during the third round of the Women's British Open (which I won by a stroke), and capped my year by holing out a pitch from a bunker at the Skins Game worth $175,000.

I've always hit a lot of fairways and greens, but now I'm confident that if I miss the green, I can still save par.

A TIGER TALE: CHIPPING WITH ONE CLUB

My chip on the 14th hole on Sunday at the McDonald's was something I never would have tried a few months earlier. Why? Because I used a lob wedge. Throughout my career I had chipped with a variety of clubs—7-iron, 9-iron, sand wedge—changing the loft depending on how much green I had to use. Nowadays, I almost always chip with my lob wedge. The impetus for the change was Tiger. We were practicing together in Orlando several weeks prior to the Colonial and I noticed that he was chipping primarily with his lob wedge. So I asked him, "Do you always chip with that?"

Then he showed me the adjustments necessary to hit a lob wedge high and low—how to alter the face to produce the different trajectories—and before long he had me sold. Then I noticed the guys at the Colonial chipping with one club, and that only reinforced my belief that Tiger's approach could work for me, too.

That was the biggest change I've made to my game in recent years. It might be easier to chip with various clubs—and I strongly advise most amateurs to do so—but I have better feel with my lob wedge. I can be more aggressive and make the ball check up, whereas with a 7-iron it felt like I was hitting a putt. I was too passive. Some of my chips stopped 10 feet short. Now I'm always around the hole, and I'm chipping better than ever.

• •

Tiger Woods and I discuss strategy during the 2001 Battle at Bighorn in Palm Desert, California. On Tiger's suggestion, I started chipping exclusively with my lob wedge in 2003. I found I could be more aggressive with one club, and I've been chipping better ever since.

FLIGHT-TO-ROLL RATIO

Chipping with several clubs, keeping the landing area the same while changing clubs depending on the amount of roll required, is still the most reliable method for the average golfer. Being able to chip consistently with only one club requires a lot of practice—you must adjust your setup constantly, and develop a feel for the length of swing that will carry the ball the right distance. Using a variety of different clubs, your setup, ball position, and swing remain relatively the same; all that changes is the club.

How does it work? First, choose your landing area. It should be a relatively flat spot about three feet onto the green. Never land the ball on the fringe or any uneven surface; the ball might stop or jump off-line.

Next, pace off the distance from the ball to the landing area, and then the distance from the landing area to the hole. In this photo, it's about five paces to the landing area (I've designated it with a towel), and another ten to the hole. That's five parts carry to ten parts roll; a 1:2 ratio. Using the flight-to-roll formula my coach Henri Reis taught me, the club of choice would be a 7-iron. Here's how it works: A sand wedge has a 2:1 ratio (two parts carry, one part roll), a 9-iron 1:1, and a 7-iron 1:2. (These are the three clubs I use to chip with;

Being able to chip consistently with only one club requires a lot of practice—you must adjust your setup constantly, and develop a feel for the length of swing that will carry the ball the right distance.

Henri suggests that beginners chip with only three clubs so as not to be confused by six or seven different ratio combinations.)

The idea is to get the ball rolling on the green as soon as possible, so it can behave like a putt. For the amateur golfer, it's usually easier to control a shot if it's on the ground.

· ·

When chipping, the object is to get the ball rolling on the green as soon as possible. I prefer using one club, but most amateurs will get better results chipping with a variety of different clubs. Why? The landing area— roughly three feet onto the putting surface (pictured here as a towel)—and swing remain fairly constant; all that changes is the club.

BASIC CHIP:
THE LOW RUNNER

Trajectory is key to controlling distance around the green. When you have a lot of green to work with, you want to play a low shot that rolls most of the way. To produce this low-running shot, choose a club according to the flight-to-roll ratio and play the ball back in your stance, just inside your right heel. Your arms and club should form a small letter "y," with your hands in front of the clubhead and your weight favoring your left side. From here, simply rock your shoulders back and forth as if you were putting, maintaining the "y" into the finish. Keep your head still, your elbows soft, and your wrists firm, and accelerate the clubhead through the ball. The club will sweep the ball off the ground and propel it toward the target.

The farther you have to carry the ball, the more your wrists should hinge in the backswing. But remember to keep your hands in front of the clubhead through impact. You must deliver a crisp, slightly descending blow, providing just enough height to get your ball to the green, where it will release and roll.

• • • • • • • • • • • • • • • • • • • •

To hit your basic chip shot, play the ball back in your stance with your hands in front of the clubhead. Your arms and shaft should form a small letter "y." Maintain this "y" throughout the swing, keeping your wrists firm and hands ahead at all times.

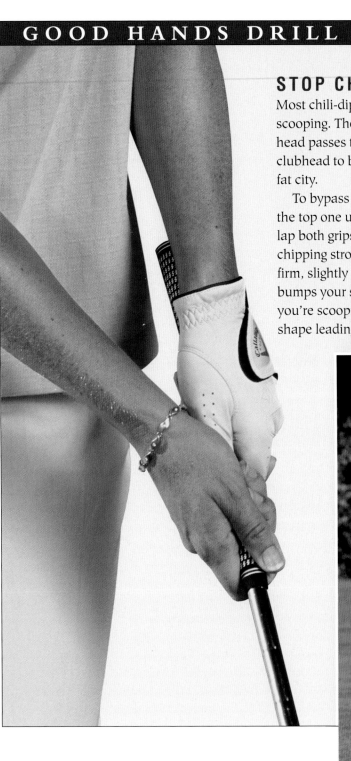

STOP CHUNKING IT

Most chili-dips, or chunked chips, result from scooping. The left wrist breaks down and the club-head passes the hands prematurely, causing the clubhead to bottom out behind the ball. Result: fat city.

To bypass fat city, try this drill. Hold two clubs, the top one upside-down so that your hands overlap both grips (*below*), and make your normal chipping stroke. Keep the back of your left wrist firm, slightly ahead of the ball (*left*). If the top shaft bumps your side, your left wrist is collapsing and you're scooping. If it doesn't, then you're in good shape leading with your hands through impact.

READ IT, FEEL IT

Since a chip spends most of its time on the ground, you should read it just like a putt. First, get a feel for the terrain with your feet as you pace off the distance between the landing area and the hole. Is it uphill or downhill? Hard or soft? If it's soft, you'll want to fly the ball closer to the hole. If the green is lightning-fast or downhill, you may want to land the ball in the fringe to take some of the speed off, or try a high, soft shot.

Once you've gauged the green's firmness, walk to a spot halfway to the hole, on the low side (*above*). From this vantage point, you can see more of the green's subtle breaks. Imagine the shot landing and rolling to the hole, and then walk back to the ball.

As you stand over the ball, focus on where you want it to land. If you've prepared correctly, you have a good chance to knock it close or make it.

FAIRWAY WOOD CHIP

Sometimes, the club of choice isn't so obvious. Consider a ball lying a foot or less from the fringe of the green, in moderate rough. I had to consider this lie on the 71st hole of the 1995 U.S. Women's Open at The Broadmoor in Colorado Springs. Trailing Meg Mallon by five shots heading into the final round, I rallied to forge a three-shot lead on the back nine. But bogeys on 15 and 16 had cut my lead to one and I was in desperate need of a par. After my third shot found the rough behind the green on the par-5 17th, it looked like I was headed for a third straight bogey. But then I hit what, for me, was the shot of the tournament: a chip-and-run that settled five feet from the hole. I saved par, then I made another par on the final hole to capture my first LPGA Tour victory and major championship.

On that particular chip, I used my putter. But times change. Today, I'd probably choose my 4- or 7-wood, a method popular among tour players right now. A fairway metal's bigger clubhead slides through tall grass more easily than a wedge or putter.

I play this shot like a normal chip, the lone difference being that I grip all the way down to the shaft. This shortens the club to the length of a putter or wedge, for better control. I position the ball back in my stance, just inside my right heel, keeping my hands ahead of the clubhead. Then, I make a chipping stroke, maintaining the "y" created by the arms and club at address. The greater mass in the clubhead transfers more energy to the ball, helping it glide through the grass and fringe like a normal putt.

GRASS ROOTS

Three things should tell you what club to use around the green. We've already discussed two of them—how much green you have to work with, and how fast the green is. Then there's the lie. If you have a clean lie, you can proceed with the flight-to-roll formula, assuming the green is fairly flat. But if the ball is nestled down in the grass, as in this photo (*right*), you'll need a more-lofted club, such as a sand or lob wedge.

From greenside rough, I position the ball farther back in my stance, opposite the big toe of my right foot, and make a normal chipping stroke. The clubhead should cut under the ball, popping it out. Because there's

grass between clubface and ball, the shot will come out with less spin—so plan for a shot that rolls farther.

• • • • • • • • • •

The fairway wood is a good option from just off the fringe. Use your normal chipping stroke, gripping down on the shaft for more control.

BELLY ON THE BUTTON

When the ball is resting up against the collar of the green, you have several options. You could chip it, but you might stub the clubhead in the grass. You could putt it, but it's hard to slide the putterhead through heavy grass. The best option? Try a bellied wedge.

Using your sand or pitching wedge, line the leading edge of the clubface up with the equator—or belly—of the ball. Set up as you would for a normal chip: ball back, hands ahead, weight favoring your front side. Make a level putting stroke. The sole of the club should only brush the top of the grass; you musn't hit down on the ball. A level path ensures that the club's leading edge strikes the middle of the ball. The ball rolls like a putt.

Line the leading edge of the clubface up with the ball's equator (*above*) and make a level putting stroke (*left*), brushing only the top of the grass.

THE STANDARD PITCH

I brought out the towel again to show you the difference between a chip and a pitch. While the landing area is the same—about three feet onto the putting surface—the distance to the towel has changed. Now I need to fly the ball farther to land it on the green. This is the standard pitch—a shot that carries about halfway to the hole and rolls the other half.

The pitch is a shorter version of my normal swing, with a few minor adjustments. First, I move my feet closer together, moving more weight to my front side. I open my stance so that my body points slightly left of the target, and I center the ball between my heels. Then I swing back and through to about waist height, allowing my wrists to hinge and unhinge. As I swing through, I turn my hips, arms, chest, and shoulders together so they all face the target at the end of the swing.

To pitch the ball farther, I speed up my body's rotation, making sure to keep everything moving together. I do not want the clubface to turn over. It should point skyward well into the follow-through.

• •

On your standard pitch, swing the club back to about waist height (*left*), allowing your wrists to hinge some. Rotate your hips, arms, and shoulders through together so your chest faces the target at the completion of the swing (*right*). The clubface should point to the sky in the follow-through. For a longer shot, speed up your body's rotation.

LOW PITCH

STANDARD PITCH

PITCHING HIGHS AND LOWS

Adjusting the height of a pitch shot is simply a matter of changing ball position. To hit a low shot that releases when it hits the green, move the ball back in your stance—opposite your right foot—and set your hands farther ahead. To hit a medium-trajectory shot, center the ball between your heels. To hit a high, soft pitch, play the ball slightly forward of center, keeping your hands almost in line with the ball.

The length of the follow-through shouldn't change. You want your hands to finish just below chest height. The biggest mistake you can make is to decelerate the clubhead into the ball. You want to keep your body moving through the shot—that's why the length of your backswing and follow-through should mirror each other.

......
Play the ball just forward of center to hit a high pitch.

HIGH
PITCH

PITCHING DRILL

HEEL YOUR PITCHES

In pitching, the clubhead should strike the ground just under the ball, letting the loft of the club send the ball skyward. But many golfers try to lift the ball, flipping their wrists to add loft.

To promote the correct downward blow, have someone lift his or her shoe as shown, and try to drive the clubhead into the bottom of his or her heel, so that the face sticks under the heel. If you scoop, the clubhead will come up early and make contact higher up.

The high floater, also called a lob, is a difficult shot for amateurs because it requires hours of practice and courage. By courage, I mean the guts to make a long, lazy swing, which is tough to do when there's so little distance between you and the hole.

Choose your most-lofted club and take a

LEARN THE LOB

Sometimes, you don't have the luxury of keeping the ball along the ground. You have to carry the rough, a bunker, or some other obstacle, and stop the ball quickly. In the photo above, my distance to the landing area (shown by the towel) is considerable. To knock it close, I need to hit a high, soft shot that flies most of the way to the hole and rolls only a few feet.

· ·

Take a slightly wider stance than normal when hitting a lob, playing the ball opposite your left heel (*right*). Swing your hands back to 10 o'clock (*above*), calmly accelerating the club into a high finish position.

TEE IT UP

The lob shot isn't something you should experiment with on the course. If you haven't practiced it, don't try it. It may look cool, but executing one gorgeous lob for every 10 attempts isn't worth all the strokes it might cost you if you fail.

When you get around to practicing it, try teeing the ball up and hitting lobs that way. Tee a ball a half-inch off the ground and make a long, flowing swing. Imagine that you're cutting the legs out from under the ball. Hit 10 balls this way, then transport this same feeling to lob shots from the rough, sweeping the clubhead through impact. Keep your hands even with the clubhead, letting the clubface slide right under the ball and projecting it almost straight up in the air.

slightly wider stance than normal. This helps lock your lower body in place, so you don't slide back and forth as much. Position the ball forward—opposite your left heel—and open your stance and clubface (the higher the shot, the more you open your clubface and body).

Now, swing your hands back to 10 o'clock, cocking your wrists. Calmly accelerate the clubhead through impact, finishing with your hands at 2 o'clock. A high finish promotes an earlier release, with your wrists swinging the clubhead upward just after impact.

CATCH A SNOWFLAKE

On a lob shot, the clubface should point upward well into the follow-through. I keep my right palm pointing straight up to the sky in my follow-through, as if I were catching a snowflake. The position of the right palm mirrors that of the clubface, so the higher the shot, the longer I keep that hand turned toward the sky.

. . . .

Point your right palm toward the sky in your follow-through to hit a high, soft lob.

ANNIKA'S KEYS TO THE SHORT GAME

I am a much more aggressive player than I used to be. Why? Because I have a better short game. I know that if I go for the green in two on a par-5 and come up short, I can still get up and down for birdie. The short game is where I save strokes. It's a major reason I was able to complete the career grand slam in 2003.

- Chip with one club if you have enough practice time. Otherwise, use various clubs, keeping the length of swing fairly constant.
- Let your hands lead the chipping stroke, maintaining the "y" formed by the arms and shaft at address.
- When pitching, swing the club back and through to waist height, keeping the clubface pointing skyward.
- Adjust the trajectory of your pitches by changing ball position—opposite your right foot for low shots, slightly forward of center for high shots.
- To pitch the ball high and soft, take a full swing under the ball and keep your right palm pointing toward the sky well into your follow-through.
- On lob shots, take a slightly wider stance than normal, distributing your weight equally on both feet.

Bunker Play

HOW TO GET OUT OF THE SAND

I track every statistic imaginable on my computer, including percentage of fairways and greens hit; times I get up and down in two shots from less than 100 yards; and percentage of sand saves. The sand has been a particular nemesis of mine over the years. Now, thankfully, I don't visit the beach all that much. In 2002, I hit my ball into only 49 greenside bunkers all year! But I got up and down only 19 of those times, for a sand-save stat of 39 percent. For me, that's not good. Had I gotten up and down a few more times, I might have won another tournament or two.

After the 2002 season, I made a commitment to improve my bunker play, much like I'd done with my putting a few years earlier. One of my goals for 2003 was to convert at least half of my sand-save chances. And that's what I did—right on the number—50 percent. Most important, some of those saves helped me capture a major championship.

Tied with Grace Park during the final round of the 2003 McDonald's LPGA Championship, I saved par with greenside bunker shots on holes 11 and 15. Then, after Grace birdied No. 17 to take a one-shot lead, I hit my second shot on the par-5 16th into the right greenside bunker, 30 yards from the pin. Using my lob wedge, I landed the ball about six feet short of the pin and put the brakes on it. The ball skipped once and checked up perfectly, two feet from the hole, for a tap-in birdie. Three holes later, after a playoff on 18, I had my first McDonald's title. Without those three sand shots, Grace would have won the tournament.

It's funny—I used to *hate* making that walk down into a bunker. Now, I've got good memories to keep me company—and keep me positive. Now I *expect* to get the ball up and down.

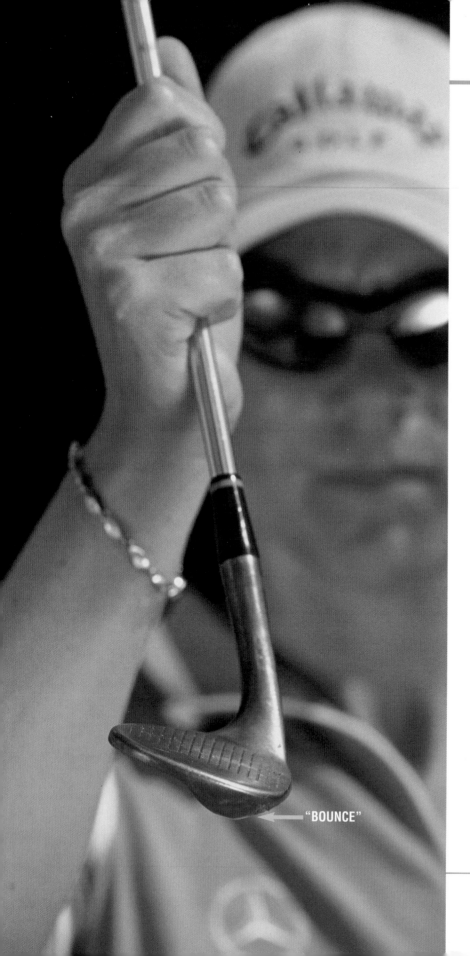

"BOUNCE"

THE BOUNCE FACTOR

To escape from greenside bunkers, you must understand the sand wedge's design and how it is meant to be used. Unlike the rest of your irons, the sand wedge has a thick, protruding sole that extends below the clubhead's leading edge. This thick trailing edge—also called "bounce"—is designed to enter the sand before the leading edge. It helps the club glide through the sand, cutting a shallow swath about the size of a dollar bill under the ball.

The clubhead should enter the sand an inch or two behind the ball. It should move smoothly through the sand, and exit a few inches past the ball. The sand wedge never strikes the ball directly; it projects the ball out on a cushion of sand.

· · · · · · · · · · · · · · · · · · ·

The sand wedge was designed so the clubhead's trailing edge, also known as "bounce," enters the sand before its leading edge. Provided that the bounce touches down first, the clubhead should glide smoothly through the sand, projecting the ball out on a cushion of sand.

MAKE A SPLASH

To get a feel for how the bounce works, lay a rake down in a bunker so that the shaft faces you. Take some swings at the rake, "bouncing" the club's trailing edge off the wooden shaft. To do this, you must keep the clubhead swinging forward. If it stops, you're swinging too steep, and you're liable to scratch or break the rake.

After hitting the rake a few times, move it aside and make the same swing in the sand, making sure the club's trailing edge touches down first. Then add a ball and repeat, rotating your body through the shot so the clubhead continues to accelerate through the sand. You should hear a loud "thump" at impact—the sound the bounce makes when it splashes into the sand.

FIRST THINGS FIRST: OPEN THE FACE

If you're anything like my pro-am playing partners, you dread being in a bunker. You're just happy to get the ball out, no matter where it finishes on the green. But there's a better way.

Using your right hand, rotate the clubface open so that it points slightly right of the target. Now add the left hand to your grip, keeping the grooves on the clubface pointing toward the sky. You want the face to remain open, exposing the bounce and helping you slide the club through the sand.

· ·

Rotate the face open with your right hand (*far left*) before taking your grip, making sure that the grooves on the face continue to point skyward (*left*).

Set up as if you were going to hit a big slice, aligning your feet, hips, and shoulders left of the flag (*left*), and playing the ball forward in your stance, just off your left heel (*above*). Swing down along your body line, accelerating the clubhead through the sand (*right*).

CUT ACROSS THE BALL

In the sand, I play the ball forward in my stance, just inside my left heel, and open my feet, hips, and shoulders until they're pointing left of the target. (The clubface should point at the flag.) My stance is a little wider than normal and my knees more flexed, which steadies the lower body so I can use more of my upper body in the shot. Lowering my body also encourages the clubhead to slide underneath the

ball, propelling it high and soft, without releasing the ball too much.

I take the club back about three-quarters, just as I would on a full wedge shot, and then swing down along my stance line, contacting the sand behind the ball. Because the clubhead is open relative to the swing path, the ball will come out with some "cut" spin. Expect it to roll a little from left to right after landing on the green.

TURN YOUR SHOULDERS THROUGH

If there's one swing thought I use in a bunker, it's "turn the shoulders through." My tendency has always been to use my hands and arms too much on sand shots, which makes the clubface turn over and dig, producing a low ball-flight and too much roll. It's better to fly the ball most of the way to the hole, using backspin to make it check up.

To hit a high, soft sand shot, you must keep the clubface pointing skyward through impact. How? I simply turn my shoulders through to the finish, rotating my upper torso through the shot until my chest points left of the target. My hands stay in front of my body well into the follow-through, keeping the clubface open.

To hit a high, soft shot, keep the clubface pointing skyward through impact, turning your shoulders through to the finish.

DIG IT

The first thing to do when you enter a bunker is examine your lie. How is the ball sitting? Is the sand firm or soft? How high is the lip? Most golfers just grab a sand wedge and flail away, but that's the wrong approach.

Consider the texture of the sand. Depending on what part of the country you're in, it can vary a lot. If you're playing a course for the very first time, hit a few shots from a practice bunker to see how the club and ball react to the sand. Typically, the finer or fluffier the sand, the more the clubhead will dig. To combat this, I open the face more, increasing the angle of the bounce (*above*).

In coarse, heavy sand, the clubhead tends to bounce off the surface. So I square the clubface more—in some cases, even close it slightly—so it can dig in. If the sand is hard and wet, I'll put a little more of my weight on my left side and square the clubface before making my normal bunker swing.

MADE IN THE SHADES

You'll notice that I often wear my Oakley sunglasses on the course. It's not to block out the spectators—I enjoy playing in front of the fans. But the sun makes me squint, and squinting makes a player tense up. You can't be tense if you want to hit a successful bunker shot; you need your arms and shoulders to swing freely.

Sand reflects sunlight strongly, and it can get almost blinding in a white-sand bunker. Sunglasses help reduce the glare.

SHORT SHOT, SHORT FINISH

Because most amateurs struggle with sand shots, I suggest they make a full follow-through, which keeps the clubhead accelerating through the sand. But for an extremely short bunker shot— say 10 yards or less—you may want to abbreviate your finish. On these shots, I cut off my follow-through so that my hands finish at waist height. The shorter the follow-through, the less speed the clubhead has as it moves through the sand. If the pin is in the middle of the green, I'll swing my hands to about chest-height. If it's way back, I'll swing into a full finish, with my hands moving above my left shoulder.

As you practice your bunker shots, try controlling the distance this way. Keep your backswing the same, but follow through to various spots. You'll find your bunker shots easier to control.

· ·

I regulate the distance of most greenside bunker shots with my follow-through. If the pin is fairly close, I swing my hands to about waist height; in the middle, to chest-height (*right*); way back, over my left shoulder.

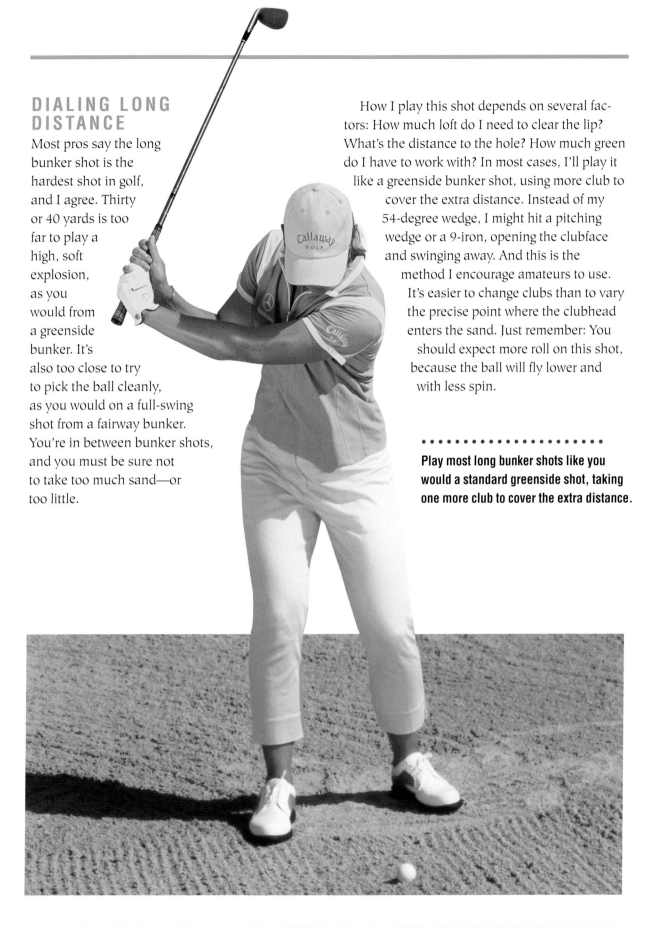

DIALING LONG DISTANCE

Most pros say the long bunker shot is the hardest shot in golf, and I agree. Thirty or 40 yards is too far to play a high, soft explosion, as you would from a greenside bunker. It's also too close to try to pick the ball cleanly, as you would on a full-swing shot from a fairway bunker. You're in between bunker shots, and you must be sure not to take too much sand—or too little.

How I play this shot depends on several factors: How much loft do I need to clear the lip? What's the distance to the hole? How much green do I have to work with? In most cases, I'll play it like a greenside bunker shot, using more club to cover the extra distance. Instead of my 54-degree wedge, I might hit a pitching wedge or a 9-iron, opening the clubface and swinging away. And this is the method I encourage amateurs to use. It's easier to change clubs than to vary the precise point where the clubhead enters the sand. Just remember: You should expect more roll on this shot, because the ball will fly lower and with less spin.

Play most long bunker shots like you would a standard greenside shot, taking one more club to cover the extra distance.

ONE SHOT FOR $175,000

There are exceptions to the rule. One of the most memorable shots in Skins Game history—and under the circumstances, probably the best single shot I've ever hit—was a 39-yard bunker shot I holed out for an eagle at the 2003 Skins Game.

That was a thrilling day for me, being the first woman ever to play in the nationally televised Skins Game on Thanksgiving weekend. Playing the par-5, 524-yard 9th hole at Trilogy Golf Club in La Quinta, California, with four skins and $175,000 on the line, I hit my tee shot into the left rough. Since I had no chance to win the hole with a birdie, I figured my best chance for eagle was to land my approach in the left greenside bunker and hole it from there.

But instead of hitting the ball into the greenside bunker, I left my 7-wood approach in the worst possible place—another bunker about 40 yards short and right of the green. Given the shot's degree of difficulty, I would have been extremely happy to get the ball within 10 feet of the cup. Too bad a 10-foot putt for birdie would do me no good with the competition—Fred Couples, Phil Mickelson, and Mark O'Meara—I faced.

I had a decent lie. The ball was resting on an upslope and the bunker lip wasn't much of a factor. I also had plenty of green to work with, so I opted to play it like a pitch-and-run—positioning the ball farther back in my stance to ensure ball-first contact, and setting my hips and shoulders parallel to the slope. Using my 54-degree sand wedge, I picked the ball clean, hardly disturbing the sand. The ball landed on

That was definitely a shot I'll never forget. Couples called it "absolutely perfect." He said you could be there until 8:30 the next morning, and not hit that shot again.

top of the ridge, just as I'd hoped, skipped a few times, and rolled like a putt, right toward the hole. As it got closer and closer, I began to think, *Hey, it might go in!* And amazingly, it did, winning me the four skins and $175,000. I was in shock. That was definitely a shot I'll never forget. Couples called it "absolutely perfect." He said you could be there until 8:30 the next morning, and not hit that shot again.

· ·

I was "California dreaming" after holing a bunker shot from 40 yards out at the 2003 Skins Game (*left*). The eagle was worth four skins and $175,000.

THE SAND SHOT...UNPLUGGED

On the Tuesday of my week at Colonial, I played a practice round with Sergio Garcia and my fellow countryman Jesper Parnevik. I had played with Jesper in the JCPenney Classic, but this was my first chance to tee it up with Sergio. What impressed me most about his game was his imagination around the greens. He could get it up and down from anywhere.

On the 7th hole, I hit my approach into a greenside bunker and promptly skulled the ball over the green into another bunker. After blasting out a few times, Sergio offered me a tip. He told me not to open the face so much on plugged and "fried-egg" lies, in which the ball sits in its own hole, forming a crater of sand around it (*above*). "You want the face more square, so the clubhead will dig underneath the ball," he said. I took Sergio's advice, and on the very next hole made a nice up-and-down from a lousy lie.

With a change in the position of the face, such shots aren't all that hard. When hitting from a fried-egg lie, I move the ball back in my stance—just forward of center—then square the clubface and aim about a half-inch behind the ball (I normally hit about an inch behind the ball, but with this shot there's a wall of sand around the ball, so I hit a little closer and take less sand). From here, it's a typical explosion shot. I swing to a full finish, which helps me accelerate the clubhead through the sand and "throw" the ball out.

LIP SERVICE

There are few more painful sights than discovering your ball under the lip of a bunker. But there is some good news: You get to take your frustration out on the sand. Brace your body by anchoring your left foot on the slope, and set your knees, hips, and shoulders parallel to the slope. Grip down a few inches for a steeper, more descending blow, and set the clubface square. Now make a three-quarter-length back-swing, driving the clubhead straight down into the sand just behind the ball. The leading edge of the clubhead will bull-doze its way into the sand, powering the ball up and out.

Consider using a pitching wedge or 9-iron to hit this shot. With less bounce than your sand or lob wedge, they are better diggers.

· · · · · · · · · · · · · · · ·

To get out from under a lip, grip down several inches on the club, square the face, and drive the leading edge of the clubhead into the sand behind the ball. Don't worry about any follow-through; just power the ball up and out.

STEP THROUGH ON DOWNHILL SHOTS

Having one foot out of a bunker is awkward. So is leaving yourself on a downslope—gravity will pull you toward the target. The solution? Let it. If you try to fight gravity by leaning back, more often than not you'll hit the ball fat or skull it over the green.

From this lie, I play the ball slightly behind the middle of my stance, flexing my knees and setting my hips and shoulders parallel to the slope. I open the clubface to add loft and put the majority of my weight on my front foot. Then, I take the club back on a steeper than usual plane and swing down along the slope. And after making contact, I let myself go. My right foot walks through the shot, just as a baseball pitcher strides

after releasing the ball. The extra step moves the bottom of the swing's arc forward, so I don't take too much sand behind the ball. It also allows me to carry my momentum forward, which keeps the clubhead accelerating.

With a shot this difficult, you should be happy to get out of the bunker. If you leave yourself a makeable putt, consider it a bonus.

• •

On a downslope, set your hips and shoulders parallel to the slope and let gravity take over. After making contact, stride forward with your right foot. The extra step allows you to carry your momentum forward so you continue to accelerate the clubhead through the sand. If you try and stay back, you're liable to take too much sand behind the ball.

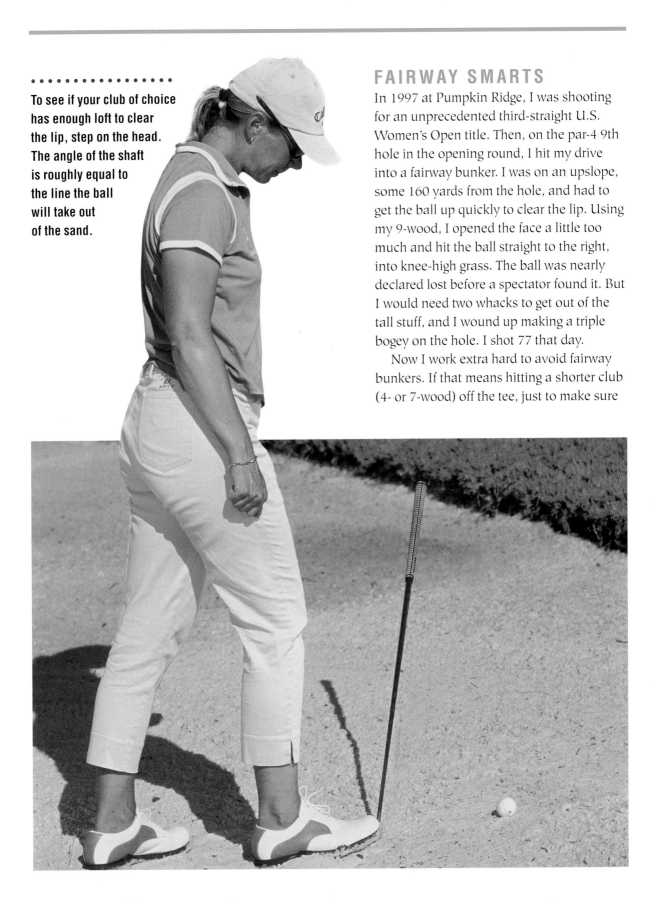

To see if your club of choice has enough loft to clear the lip, step on the head. The angle of the shaft is roughly equal to the line the ball will take out of the sand.

FAIRWAY SMARTS

In 1997 at Pumpkin Ridge, I was shooting for an unprecedented third-straight U.S. Women's Open title. Then, on the par-4 9th hole in the opening round, I hit my drive into a fairway bunker. I was on an upslope, some 160 yards from the hole, and had to get the ball up quickly to clear the lip. Using my 9-wood, I opened the face a little too much and hit the ball straight to the right, into knee-high grass. The ball was nearly declared lost before a spectator found it. But I would need two whacks to get out of the tall stuff, and I wound up making a triple bogey on the hole. I shot 77 that day.

Now I work extra hard to avoid fairway bunkers. If that means hitting a shorter club (4- or 7-wood) off the tee, just to make sure

I don't reach them, so be it. I'd rather be short and in the fairway than long and in the bunker.

If, by some miscalculation or bad bounce, I find myself in a fairway bunker, the first thing I do is make sure I have enough loft to clear the lip. If it's 160 yards to the flag but my normal 7-iron won't carry the ridge, I won't chance it: I'll blast out with a wedge and leave myself a full wedge in.

How do you know if a club has enough loft to clear the lip? To check, step on the head of the club you plan to use. (I'm demonstrating here in a bunker, but should you do this during actual play, stand outside the bunker). The angle of the shaft is roughly equal to the line the ball will take when leaving the sand. If the shaft is pointing into the lip, go to a club with more loft.

Widen your stance, knock your knees in a little bit, and dig your feet firmly into the sand. Play the ball in the middle of your stance, setting your hands forward, and grip down about an inch. Take one more club than usual for a shot of this distance—as long as it will clear the lip—and make your normal swing. Provided you make these setup adjustments and swing to a full finish, you should escape cleanly.

ANNIKA'S KEYS TO BUNKER PLAY

There was a time I dreaded the walk down into the bunker. Now, I don't mind so much. I would have never won the 2003 McDonald's LPGA Championship if not for three up-and-downs from the sand on the 11th, 15th, and 16th holes during Sunday's final round. I've improved dramatically in this area, and so can you.

- The sand wedge is designed so that the club's trailing edge—or bounce—strikes the surface before the leading edge.
- Opening the clubface exposes the bounce, which helps the clubhead glide—not dig—through the sand.
- To hit the ball high and soft, turn your shoulders so that your chest faces left of the target at the finish.
- On long bunker shots, take more club and swing normally, making sure to open the face.
- Square the face when you need the club to dig, such as when the ball is plugged or in a "fried-egg" lie.
- Always make sure you have enough loft to clear the lip of a bunker.

Putting

NEVER THREE-PUTT AGAIN

Growing up in Sweden, all I did was hit balls. In the winter, I hit balls indoors. In the summer, outside on the range. I didn't pay much attention to my putting or my short game, and it took me a long time to realize their importance.

With putting, the light finally came on after the 2000 season. While I won five times that year, my scoring average increased .07 strokes from the year before. And, for the second year in a row, I finished behind Karrie Webb for both the Rolex Player of the Year and Vare Trophy titles. It wasn't that I was hitting the ball poorly, I just wasn't making any putts. My putting average that year, 30.41, was the worst of my career, and it ranked 122nd on the LPGA Tour.

Like me, Karrie has always been an excellent ball striker. She hits a lot of greens. But watching her win three majors and 13 tournaments in 1999 and 2000, it was easy to see why: She made putts. If I was going to keep up with her, I had to start doing the same. There was no reason I couldn't be a better putter, I just had to work harder at it. So that winter, I decided to devote an extra hour a day to my putting for six straight weeks. I didn't alter my mechanics much; I just worked on speed and distance control. In a typical session I would hit 50 to 100 putts with my right hand only, and attempt to lag two dozen 30-footers to within a putter's length of the hole. If I missed, I had to start over.

My hard work paid immediate dividends. From early March to mid-April 2001, I won four straight events, including my first Nabisco Championship. As if that weren't enough, I also fired that 59 during the second round of the Standard Register PING, with only 25 total putts and 11 one-putt greens. I went on to earn $2,105,868 that year. I had learned how to "putt for dough."

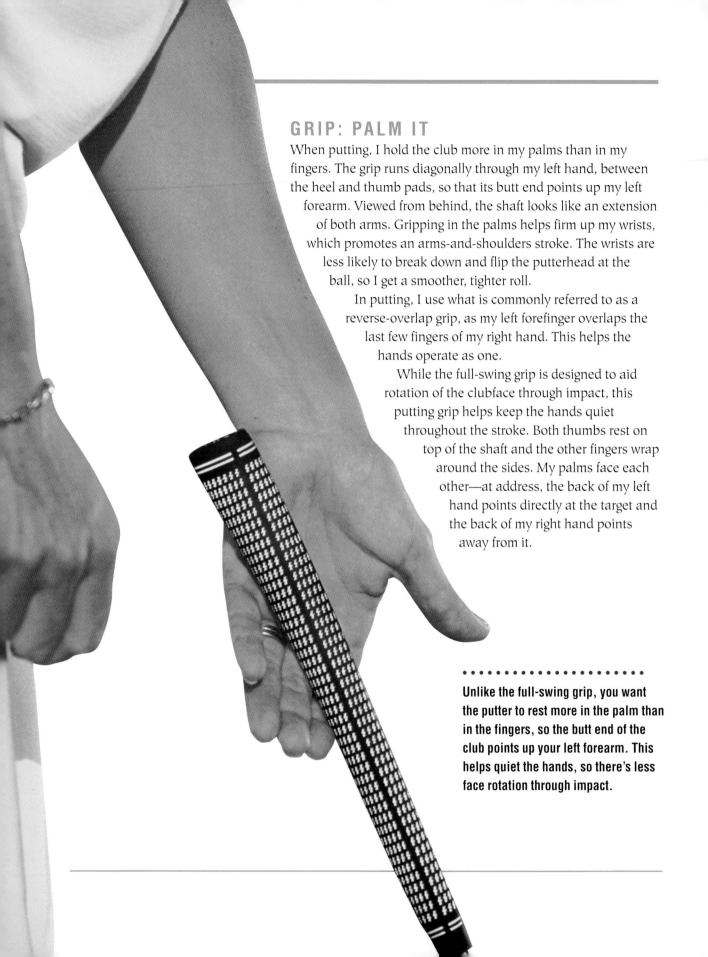

GRIP: PALM IT

When putting, I hold the club more in my palms than in my fingers. The grip runs diagonally through my left hand, between the heel and thumb pads, so that its butt end points up my left forearm. Viewed from behind, the shaft looks like an extension of both arms. Gripping in the palms helps firm up my wrists, which promotes an arms-and-shoulders stroke. The wrists are less likely to break down and flip the putterhead at the ball, so I get a smoother, tighter roll.

In putting, I use what is commonly referred to as a reverse-overlap grip, as my left forefinger overlaps the last few fingers of my right hand. This helps the hands operate as one.

While the full-swing grip is designed to aid rotation of the clubface through impact, this putting grip helps keep the hands quiet throughout the stroke. Both thumbs rest on top of the shaft and the other fingers wrap around the sides. My palms face each other—at address, the back of my left hand points directly at the target and the back of my right hand points away from it.

Unlike the full-swing grip, you want the putter to rest more in the palm than in the fingers, so the butt end of the club points up your left forearm. This helps quiet the hands, so there's less face rotation through impact.

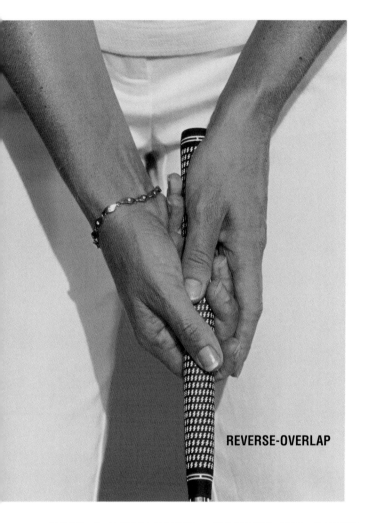

REVERSE-OVERLAP

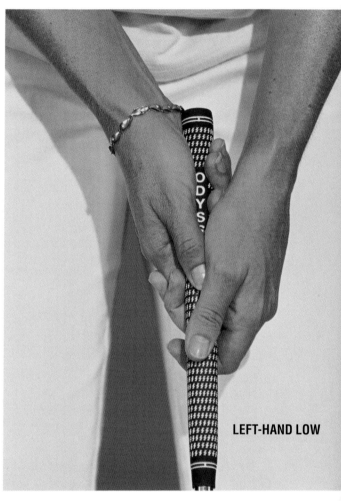

LEFT-HAND LOW

THE LOWDOWN: RIGHT OR LEFT HAND?

Throughout my career, I've switched back and forth between a conventional reverse-overlap grip and a left-hand-low (cross-handed) one. In fact, I won one major each way in 2003, capturing the McDonald's LPGA Championship with my left hand low and the Women's British Open with a conventional grip. I switched to the latter in June, just before the U.S. Open, knowing I'd face a lot of breaking putts at Pumpkin Ridge. These putts require more feel, which I get with my right hand low—as it is on my full-swing grip. Left-hand-low gives me better control over short putts, but I struggle with breaking putts and lags.

If you use a conventional grip, I still recommend that you practice occasionally with your left hand low, especially if you tend to get a little jumpy on short putts. You'll get a feel for how the back of the left hand stays flat throughout the stroke. That's a key to good putting no matter what grip you use.

GRIP PRESSURE: NOT TOO RELAXED

I hold my putter lightly: just tight enough to feel the putterhead swinging through the stroke. Any lighter and I lose my feel for the putt's speed and distance—a lesson I learned at the Colonial. In the first round, I hit all but one fairway and 14 of 18 greens in regulation, but shot a 1-over-par 71. Had I made a few putts, it could have been a 67 or 68. Nearly half my strokes that day (33) were putts.

As is my tendency when I get nervous, I left a lot of putts short, starting with a 16-foot birdie attempt on my very first hole. I was tentative all day long, and it never occurred to me that I might be gripping the putter too lightly. If anything, I was focusing on keeping my grip light because I was so nervous—if only to reduce my overall tension. But then, after the round, my swing coach Henri Reis said, "Maybe your grip is *too* relaxed. That's why you have no feel." He was right. The connection between my hands and the putter was so soft, I might as well have been swinging a pillow.

The next day I increased my grip pressure and putted much better. I told Henri, "If I had known this before, I might have won two or three more majors."

SETUP: HANDS EVEN WITH BALL

I don't normally finish bogey-bogey or shoot 76 on Sunday, but I did both during the final round of the 2002 Ping Banner Health. I three-putted from 25 feet for bogey on 17, made bogey from a bunker on 18, and eventually lost a playoff to Rachel Teske—all on the same Moon Valley

Country Club course where I'd shot 59 a year earlier. Rachel played great down the stretch, rallying from three shots back with two to play, but I helped her. In fact, I threw the tournament away. I couldn't lag my first putts close to the hole, and it cost me.

Once the playoff ended, it took me about two minutes to figure out what was wrong. My hands were too far behind the ball at address. Henri and I went to the practice green, where I moved my hands forward and immediately sank five putts in a row.

Ideally, I want my hands even with the ball— or just slightly ahead (*above*)—so the shaft is nearly vertical. Then I can make a true pendulum

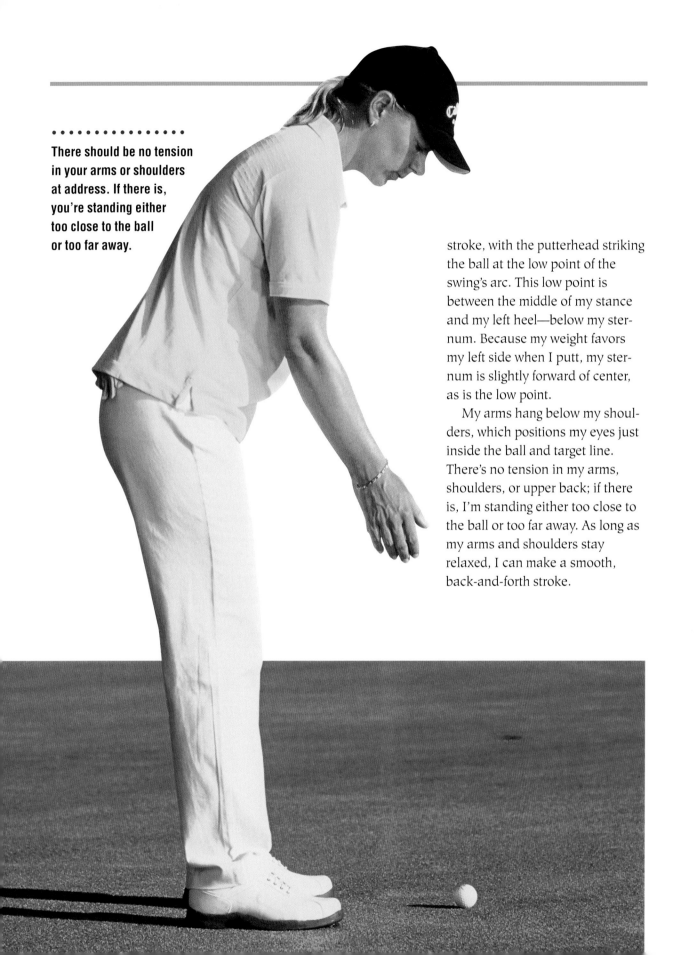

There should be no tension in your arms or shoulders at address. If there is, you're standing either too close to the ball or too far away.

stroke, with the putterhead striking the ball at the low point of the swing's arc. This low point is between the middle of my stance and my left heel—below my sternum. Because my weight favors my left side when I putt, my sternum is slightly forward of center, as is the low point.

My arms hang below my shoulders, which positions my eyes just inside the ball and target line. There's no tension in my arms, shoulders, or upper back; if there is, I'm standing either too close to the ball or too far away. As long as my arms and shoulders stay relaxed, I can make a smooth, back-and-forth stroke.

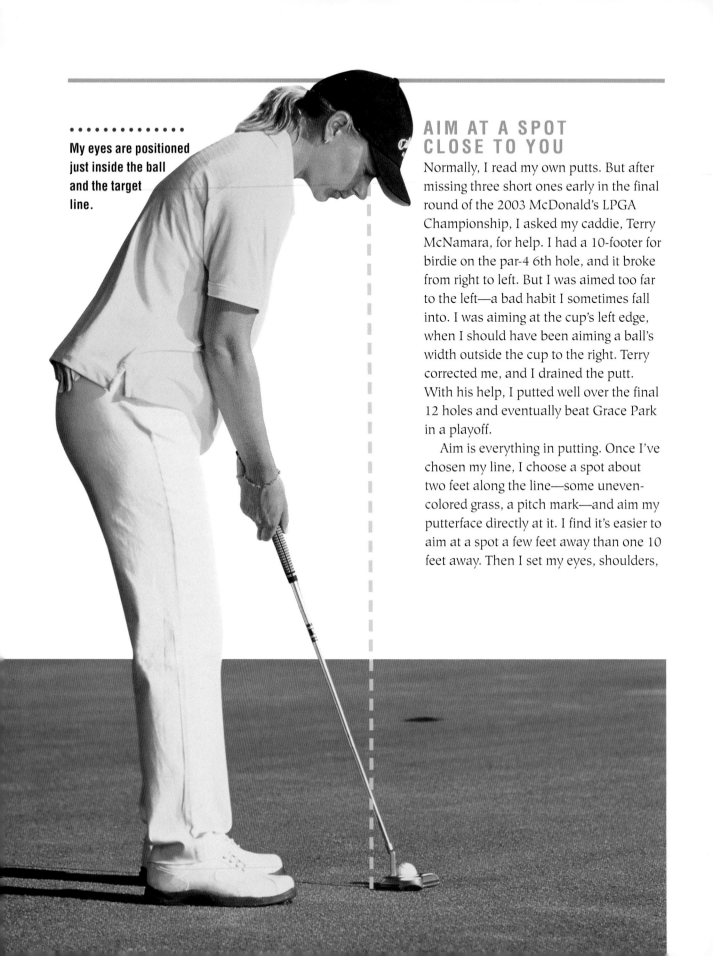

My eyes are positioned just inside the ball and the target line.

AIM AT A SPOT CLOSE TO YOU

Normally, I read my own putts. But after missing three short ones early in the final round of the 2003 McDonald's LPGA Championship, I asked my caddie, Terry McNamara, for help. I had a 10-footer for birdie on the par-4 6th hole, and it broke from right to left. But I was aimed too far to the left—a bad habit I sometimes fall into. I was aiming at the cup's left edge, when I should have been aiming a ball's width outside the cup to the right. Terry corrected me, and I drained the putt. With his help, I putted well over the final 12 holes and eventually beat Grace Park in a playoff.

Aim is everything in putting. Once I've chosen my line, I choose a spot about two feet along the line—some uneven-colored grass, a pitch mark—and aim my putterface directly at it. I find it's easier to aim at a spot a few feet away than one 10 feet away. Then I set my eyes, shoulders, hips, knees, and feet parallel to the line. My stance is slightly open, giving me a clear view of the line and the target. I'm careful not to lift my head as I take one final look at the hole—looking up could throw off my aim.

Provided I'm the correct distance from the ball—arms relaxed, eyes just inside the target line—I'm ready to begin the stroke.

PRACTICE YOUR AIM

I don't use many training aids, but the triangle shown here is terrific. Line up the center of your putterhead with the line on the triangle (the putt's initial starting line), setting the face square against the triangle. Once you get a sense of what square looks like, set your body parallel to the line on the triangle. Practice for 10 minutes a day and you'll start to feel confident about your aim. Then you can shift your attention to the speed of your putts.

If you can't find a triangle, take a Magic Marker and draw a line approximately one third of the way around the ball's circumference. Aim the stripe at the putt's starting line, and then align the putter and your body to the line on the ball.

· · · · · · · · · · · · · · · · · · ·

Once I set the face down square, I aim the center of the putterhead at the putt's initial starting line.

THE STROKE: NO PEEKING

During the Colonial, I got a phone call from an interested spectator back in Orlando—Tiger Woods. Tiger and I had chatted quite a bit in the days leading up to the Colonial, and he called after the first round to offer me some encouragement... and putting advice.

"Keep your head down," he said. "Roll the rock. You'll get right back in contention."

That's great advice for any putter. Sometimes, I have a tendency to look up early to see where the ball is going, and by lifting my head prematurely, I pull my shoulders and putter off-line. But when I "roll the rock" correctly, I don't look up until my stroke is complete and the ball is well on its way. Sometimes I'll wait to hear the ball rattling in the cup, which is as good as seeing it go in.

Otherwise, my putting stroke is very similar to a chip. I try to maintain the "y" created by my arms and club through the entire motion. I simply rock my shoulders back and through in a pendulum fashion, keeping my left elbow moving toward the target and the putterhead fairly low to the ground. My hands feel like they're leading the stroke, with the back of my left hand staying flat well into the follow-through.

The length of the backstroke determines the length of the putt. To ensure that the momentum of the backstroke is carried through impact, I make sure my forward stroke goes at least as far as my backstroke. You must accelerate the putterhead for all putts, even downhillers. Amateurs make tentative strokes on downhill putts because they're afraid the ball will roll 10 feet past the hole. Instead, shorten your stroke—the only way to keep a putt on line is to accelerate through the ball.

BREAKING PUTTS: AIM HIGH

After the 1999 U.S. Open I played in an outing with several seniors from what is now known as the Champions Tour. Having putted so poorly that I missed the cut at the Open, I was desperate for some tips. On the first day, so many of the guys came up to me on the practice green to offer advice that I had to turn them away. "Thank you," I told them, "but I need just one person." They were all in agreement on who that should be.

The next day I showed up on the practice green and, sure enough, there was only one gentleman standing there: Dave Stockton.

Stockton, who won the 1970 and '76 PGA Championships and captained the U.S. Ryder Cup team to victory at Kiawah Island in 1991, was a tremendous help. He taught me to read putts from the low side, to get a better view of the green's slope. He also taught me about speed: You want to hit every putt with just enough pace to send it a foot and a half past the hole. My most important tip from Dave, however, dealt with where the ball should enter the cup. He said to picture the hole as a clockface, and to see the ball rolling in on the high side, not straight in. Example: If a putt breaks from right to left, the ball should enter the hole at 4 or 5 o'clock, not 6.

Too many golfers aim for the center of the hole. But if you aim there, only half of the hole is available to you. If the putt has any break at all—and nearly every putt does—you will miss below the hole. But if you read the right amount of break and play for the high side of the cup, the hole seems much larger.

On breaking putts, I visualize the break and aim for the highest point along the line— that spot where the ball begins its descent toward the hole (shown by the tee in this photo). Gravity takes over from there, feeding the ball down to the hole. If my line and speed are correct, the ball should die in on the high side of the cup.

• •

Aim for the highest point along the putt's line (represented here by the tee), and let gravity feed the ball down toward the hole. Picture the putt entering on the high side of the cup, not its center.

AIM HIGH

The next time you practice, stick a tee behind the hole on an extension of the line where you see the ball entering the cup (as shown here). Take several practice putts, rolling the ball at the tee. Then remove the tee and roll several more balls, imagining that the tee is still there. Picture this tee when putting on the course in competition, too, remembering that putts break most around the hole, when they are slowing down.

The image of the tee will train you to keep the ball above the hole on breaking putts, so that it falls in on the high side. If you don't play enough break, your putts will keep missing to the low side, below the hole. And a putt can't drop if it's coming in from the low side.

READING PUTTS: GO LOW

If a putt breaks from left to right (*below*), I view it from the right side—the low side—walking halfway along the line to get an accurate read. From here, I can see the slope better than I can from the high side, where it runs away from me. I also read the putt from behind the hole, picturing the spot where I think the ball will roll in.

THE MAGIC 18

Like my driver, my putter has a speed limit. Following Dave Stockton's advice, I try to stroke every putt just hard enough so that if it misses, the ball finishes 18 inches past the cup. That way I minimize those heartbreaking, inches-short misses without leaving myself too many tough comebackers for par.

LONG DISTANCE: PUTT TO A CIRCLE

On long putts, you've got to be a good judge of distance. If your speed is right, it's almost impossible to three-putt. I divide every long putt into two segments, walking halfway to the hole and making several practice strokes there while looking from the ball to the hole. Viewing putts this way makes it easier to gauge the length and pace of my stroke.

The goal is to have an easy second putt. It's like laying up on a par-5: I want to leave myself the perfect distance for the next shot. For a putt, that means three feet or less and preferably uphill, so I can be aggressive on my next attempt. It helps to envision a circle six feet in diameter around the hole. If I can get my first putt within that circle—no more than three feet from the cup—I'll surely sink the next one.

When I read a putt, I'll pick an intermediate point about halfway to the hole and aim for that point. Then I'll picture the putt rolling over that spot. I think of the putt as I would a ski slope, envisioning the putt's trail and trying to keep the ball inside that track.

As for technique, my posture is a little more upright on long putts, which gives me a better view of the target line. The stroke is similar to a chip—longer than that of a short putt, with some lower body movement.

I take several more practice strokes behind the ball, getting a feel for the size and pace of the stroke. Then I try to repeat that feeling in my actual stroke.

From really long distance, putt like you chip. Stand a little taller than normal, and make a much longer stroke back and through, allowing your lower body to react to the movement. The goal is to give yourself an easy second putt, so anything inside three feet is a success.

LAG PUTT DRILL

PUTT TO A TEE

Practice putting to a tee 20 or 30 feet away. The object is to hit each putt with enough speed so that the ball finishes within a putter's length of the tee (*below*)—preferably beyond the tee. Don't worry about technique. Just focus on distance. Putting to a small target helps sharpen your distance control and improves your confidence. The hole will look much bigger when you're out on the course.

If you spend less time reading putts and focus more on speed, you'll be a better lag putter.

SHORT PUTTS: KEEP IT SQUARE

In 2002 I won 13 events worldwide and 11 on the LPGA Tour. A big reason was my putting, particularly from a short range. For the first time since 1997, I averaged less than 30 putts per round. But in the final tournament of the year, the ADT Tour Championship at Trump International, my putter went cold. Sure, I was 5-under after two rounds, but I had hit 33 of 36 greens. I knew I'd left a ton of putts out there.

Fortunately, my coach was in town. Henri noticed that my putter was rising too much after impact. So I worked on keeping the putterhead low in the throughstroke. It worked— I began getting a much truer roll.

As a drill, I'd drop several balls about three feet from the hole and—with no backstroke— push the ball toward the hole. This is a great drill for short putts, because it immediately tells me if I've got the putterface square to the target. If you can keep the putterface square, you'll sink most of your short putts. This drill also teaches you to extend the putterhead down the target line while keeping the face square. On short putts, you should feel like you're sticking the putterhead into the hole.

• •

The key to sinking more short putts is keeping the putterface square to the target. As a drill, drop several balls three feet from the hole and, without making a backswing, push the ball toward the hole (*left*), extending the putterhead down the target line. This will immediately tell you if the putterface is square to your line.

PRE-PUTT ROUTINE: STAND PERPENDICULAR

My pro-am playing partners are always asking me where to aim, whether it's for a three-foot putt or a 30-footer. They're so concerned with a putt's line that they forget that speed is the most important element in putting. Get your speed right, and unless a putt is several feet off-line, you'll have an easy putt coming back.

In my pre-putt routine, I try to be instinctive as well as analytical. I start behind the ball, standing perpendicular to the target line as I take my practice strokes, so I can view the whole line.

Then I take my stance, right foot first, aiming the putterface at a spot about two feet along my line. I set my feet and body parallel to the target line, take one last look at the hole—visualizing the ball going into the cup—look back at the ball, and then stroke. As with my full swing, I don't spend much time over the ball before I putt. Once I'm set, my intentions are clear. There's no room for indecision.

• •

I prefer to take my practice strokes behind the ball, standing perpendicular to the putt's initial starting line. From here, I can see the line much better than I can standing to the side of the ball. Once I get a good feel for the putt's speed, I walk into the ball and aim the face at an intermediate spot along my target line (*far right*).

TAKE AIM
Aim the clubface at a spot about
two feet along your target line.

GET SET
Set your feet and body parallel
to the putt's starting line.

GO
Take one last look at the
hole, return your eyes to
the ball and then stroke.

My putting routine involves making strokes with my right hand only (*left*), and plenty of tees (*below*).

MY PUTTING WARM-UP

If my pro-am playing partners spent as much time on the practice green as they do on the range, they'd shave five strokes off their scores. Easily. I warm up for 1 hour and 15 minutes prior to every tournament round, starting on the practice green with a putting routine I devised in 2001. I used to take three balls, putt around, and not pay much attention to the line. It was more about feel.

Now I start by hitting three-foot putts with my right hand only—50 to 100 putts—just trying to make a good stroke. Then I have my caddie put down three sets of three tees, all six to fifteen feet from the hole, with one ball at each tee. That's birdie range. I start with the short one, read the line, and try to make it. I continue around in a circle and attempt to make them all. Then I go around again for a total of 18 putts. The most I have ever made is 16 out of 18.

I follow the same putting routine every day, whether in practice or at a tournament. I start with short putts, because I want to see the ball going into the hole. The more putts you see falling in, the more confidence you'll have out on the course. I putt with my right hand only because it's the dominant hand, the one that sets the pace of the stroke. Just as warming up with a wedge programs a good tempo for my full swing, putting one-handed smooths out my stroke.

I move up to the longer putts before heading over to the chipping area to continue my warm-up. But if you have only a few minutes to warm up, you should hit several long putts, using one ball and putting out each time. This will prepare you for the pressure you'll face out on the first green.

ANNIKA'S KEYS TO PUTTING

Growing up, I didn't putt much. Like most amateurs, I spent the vast majority of my practice time hitting balls on the range. It took the worst putting year of my career to finally make me understand one of the most important rules in golf: If your putts aren't falling, you're not going to score as well as you should.

- Grip your putter more in the palm, less in the fingers. The shaft points up your left forearm.
- Position the ball at the low point of the stroke, between the middle of your stance and your left heel. Your hands should be even with the ball.
- It's all about speed: Hit each putt with enough pace so that if it misses, it finishes 18 inches past the hole.
- On breaking putts, picture the ball rolling in on the high side, not straight in.
- On long putts, pick an intermediate point about halfway to the hole and visualize the putt rolling over that spot.
- Accelerate the putter through the ball on short putts, keeping the putterhead low.

The Mental

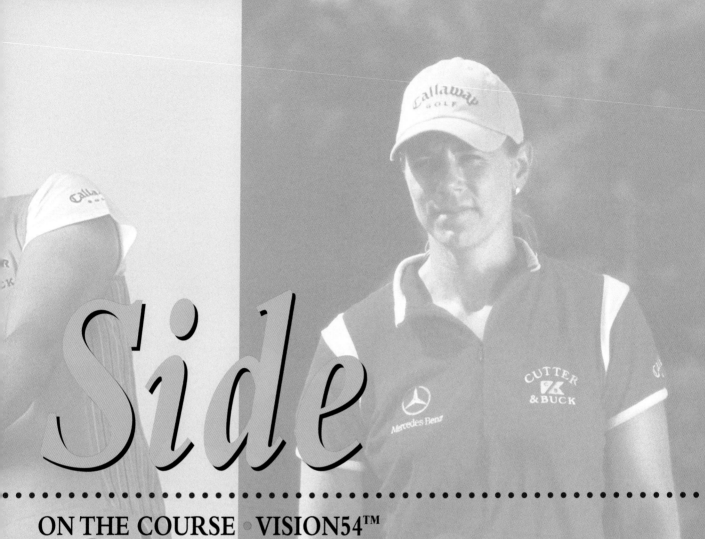

Side

···

ON THE COURSE · VISION54™

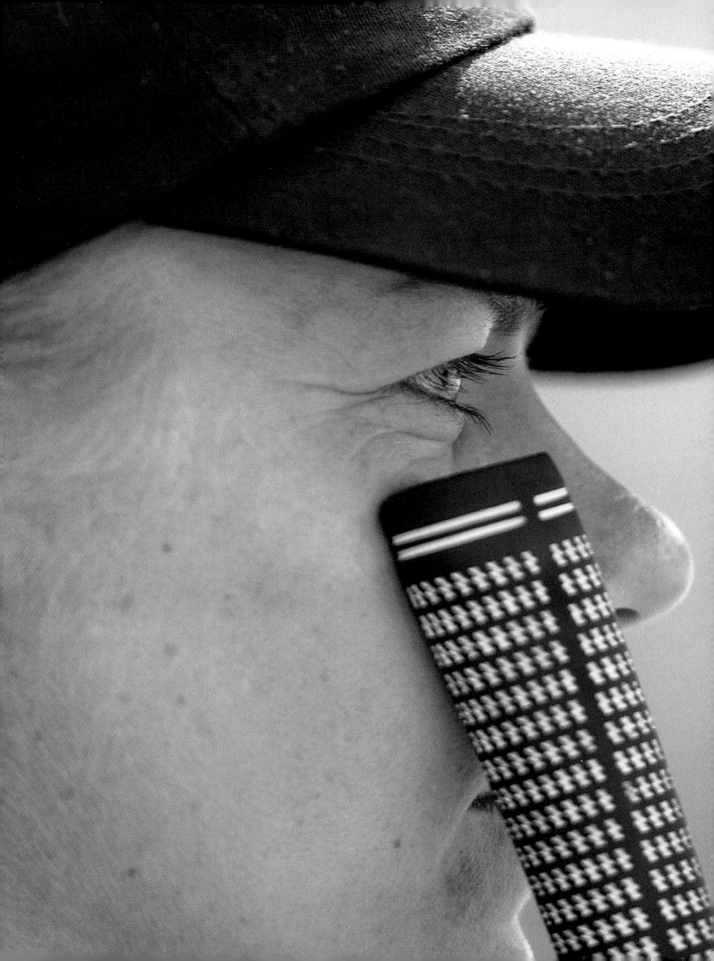

On the Course

A BEAUTIFUL MIND GAME

The 406-yard 17th hole at Royal Lytham & St. Annes Golf Club is a puzzle. The first time you play this dogleg right-to-left hole you want to hit driver. But experience says otherwise: what you can't see really can hurt you. Bunkers line both sides of the fairway—several of them fairly deep—ready to swallow any ball that strays off-line. Hitting into any of them will probably cost you a stroke.

My strategy during the 2003 Women's British Open was to play short of the bunkers, laying up with either a 7-wood or a long iron. This left me with another long club into the green, but it was the right play. In fact, during the final round, I hit a 4-iron off the tee and came up just two yards short of a fairway bunker. One more club and I would have been in the bunker. Most courses, the longer you hit it, the better off you are. Royal Lytham is not one of those courses. There are 50 bunkers alone on the last three holes, so you have to think really hard on every tee: Which direction do I take? Which club do I use?

But that kind of thinking suits one of my greatest strengths: course management. It means knowing where to hit the ball and where not to hit it. It's knowing what shots you're most comfortable hitting, and which angle will give you the best shot into the green. It's knowing when to be aggressive and when not to be, and always thinking one shot ahead.

For the week of the British Open, I played the 17th at 1-under par, sinking a 32-foot putt for birdie in the first round. I'll take 1-under par any time. I wasn't trying to repeat the heroics of Bobby Jones, who, during the 1926 British Open, drove into a fairway bunker on Lytham's 17th, only to hit a miraculous shot onto the green with his mashie from 175 yards away. I was told there's a plaque on that spot commemorating his approach, but I never saw it. I was determined not to hit my ball anywhere near that bunker.

TEE SHOTS: PLAY SHORT OF TROUBLE

For me, it's all about placement—avoiding fairway bunkers, water, and rough, and leaving myself in a good position to fire at the green. If I can carry a hazard, I will. But if I might reach the hazard with a driver, I'll take less club and play it safe.

As I played the 72nd hole of the 2003 McDonald's LPGA Championship, I was tied with Grace Park at 6-under par. The course was soaked from days of rain, so any shot in the rough would almost certainly cost me a stroke. It was essential to keep my tee shot in the fairway, so I chose my 4-wood off the tee. My tee shot sailed to the right and gave me an anxious moment, but then landed several yards short of disaster in the first cut of rough. Had I hit the driver I would have certainly been in the tall, wet grass, and probably out of a playoff—a playoff I would go on to win 20 minutes later.

Placement was just as critical off the tee at the Colonial. If I hit my driver, bunkers would come into play on most holes. The male pros could carry those bunkers, but since I didn't have their strength, I teed off with my 4-wood—five times each round—and stayed short of the sand.

It's better to be conservative and hit in the fairway than to risk going into the rough or behind a tree. As long as I'm in the short grass, I have a chance to make birdie.

• •

Off the tee, my goal is to keep the ball in the short grass. If my driver puts the fairway bunkers in play, I'll lay up short of the bunkers with a fairway wood (*left*). It's all about placement—staying out of trouble and creating the best approach into the green.

USE THE WHOLE TEE BOX

Most golfers instinctively stick their pegs in the middle of the tee box, never thinking to move to the far right or left. Before you do the same, consider the following: First of all, where's the danger? If there's a bunker or hazard on the left side of the fairway, I'll tee the ball on the far left side of the box. From this angle, it's easier to aim the other way. A second consideration is the shape of your usual shot. If you normally fade the ball, tee it up near the right marker and aim at the left side of the fairway, curving the ball back toward the center. Even if you hit it dead straight, it's likely to finish in the short grass.

Club selection also plays a role in keeping hazards out of play. In the photo below, I'm going over the water because it's an easy carry for my driver—175 yards. I'm teeing up near the left marker to play a slight draw, aiming at the flag and curving the ball back toward the center of the fairway.

But suppose it was 250 yards to carry the water. In that case, I would aim left and use less club—probably a 5-iron, because I want to stay short of the trees. I'd tee the ball near the right marker (*below*) to give myself the best angle away from the water.

As you can see, changing sides makes the hole look dramatically different. I've created the straightest possible angle to the fairway for both shots, increasing the size of my landing area.

• •

Use the whole box when teeing off, changing sides to create the widest landing area possible (*opposite page and below*). You'll hit more fairways this way.

DOGLEGS: KNOW WHERE THEY START—AND FINISH

When you face a dogleg, ask yourself: "Is there a big advantage to cutting the corner?" If it means having a short approach shot to the green instead of a long iron or wood, then go for it. But if it's only a two- or three-club difference, don't take the risk. Instead, determine the distance to the start of the dogleg (where it begins to bend) and the corner (where the fairway runs out). Choose a club that will put you safely between those two yardages.

Don't risk hitting through the dogleg. If you have 200 yards to the start of the dogleg and 230 to the corner, choose a club you can safely carry 210–215 yards, allowing for a little roll.

Also be careful not to deviate from your natural shot shape. If your tendency is to fade the ball and the hole bends from right to left, don't try to draw it around the corner. Aim at the left edge of the dogleg and curve it toward the middle of the fairway. Similarly, don't try and cut the ball from left to right if you naturally draw the ball.

MY GOLDEN RULE: 6 OUT OF 10

Throughout the 1990s, I teamed with Jesper Parnevik in the JCPenney event. He's always fun to play a round with. Once we were standing on a par-3 hole as Jesper and his caddie discussed strategy: Should he hit a low draw, a high fade, or something else? Their conversation went on until finally I said, "Why don't you just play a normal, straight shot?"

I couldn't understand why he was making it so complicated. And I'm not singling Jesper out. I think a lot of players try to hit the prettiest shot instead of the obvious one. And most of them

can hit pretty much any shot they want. But my philosophy is this: If you can hit the ball straight at the pin or right down the middle of the fairway, then do it.

Always play to your strengths. If I can pull off a difficult shot 6 times out of 10, I'll consider going for it. Anything less and I'll leave it for the practice range. The only exception is if I'm back in the pack and need to make up ground in a hurry—that's when it's time to get aggressive.

Golf is situational. The first time I played at Trump International during the 2001 ADT Tour Championship, I didn't even consider cutting the dogleg and driving the green on the par-4, 335-yard 6th hole. But after adding 13 yards to my average drive, I decided to go for it in '02. I could now carry the water (240 yards) about 9 out of 10 times. It was worth the risk because if I cleared the water, I had two shots left to make birdie and three to make par. Even if I put it in the water, I could still get up and down from the drop zone for par.

In 2003, they moved the tee up to entice everyone to go for the green. But I wasn't biting. My driver was now too much club and my 4-wood wasn't enough. So I hit an iron while many other players were reaching for their drivers. In this case, the "obvious" play wasn't right for my game.

• •

My golden rule is this: If I don't think I can hit the shot 6 times out of 10, I won't try it. In this photo, I have a difficult pitch into the green, with a bunker hugging the flag and water lurking just beyond the green. Rather than try to knock it stiff from the rough—which takes spin off the ball—I'm going to play the odds and pitch it to the middle of the green.

FIRST-TEE JITTERS

How nervous was I before my first tee shot at the Colonial playing with the men? When I tried to speak to my caddie, Terry, my mouth moved but nothing came out. I couldn't feel my arms; all I could feel were the butterflies in my stomach. How I hit the fairway, I'll never know.

Like any golfer, I get nervous on the first tee—although never to the extreme I was on that day. First-tee jitters are understandable: You want to get off to a good start and set a positive tone for your round. But you also have to realize that the first shot is not life and death. If you miss the fairway, the round isn't over. No matter what shot you hit, it's just the beginning.

At the Colonial, Terry and I had a plan for how we'd attack every hole, as we always do, but our game plan didn't include my opening tee shot. We knew that under the circumstances—all the buildup, the 10,000 pairs of eyes surrounding me on the tee, with millions more watching at home—that the shot could go anywhere. And that was okay: We'd go find it and play from there.

Fortunately, I split the fairway. Knocked it out there pretty good, too.

On the first tee, go ahead and be nervous. Most people are afraid of the jitters because they assume they'll hit a poor shot as a result. Not me. I *like* feeling nervous because I perform better that way. Things slow down and I get more *focused*.

• •

I was never more nervous teeing off than I was on No. 10 at Colonial (*left*). One of the things that helped calm my nerves was my breathing. Performed properly, it will help reduce your heart rate and your tension level.

You want to get off to a good start and set a positive tone for your round. But you also have to realize that the first shot is not life and death. If you miss the fairway, the round isn't over. No matter what shot you hit, it's just the beginning.

Another reason I hit that fairway was my preshot routine. Terry (whose legs were shaking, too) managed to clock my routine before my first shot of the Colonial at 22 seconds—right on average. I went through my normal moves (see Chapter 3 on Driving for more details), and as I stood over the ball, I turned my focus inward: I put myself in a bubble where no one could touch me, no one could see me. I imagined I was hitting a routine 4-wood on the practice range—as I've done thousands of times before—and I blocked everything else out of my mind.

That's what a good preshot routine does: It puts you in a comfort zone. It helps you calm down and zero in on the shot at hand. It helps you focus on the shot of your life under the most intense pressure imaginable, and swing as smoothly as if you were playing alone.

BREATHE IN, BREATHE OUT

Another thing helped me on the tee at the Colonial: my breathing. People tend to breathe really fast when they're nervous, and I was no different that day. But I knew what to do. As I take my stance over the ball, I take a deep breath—starting at my diaphragm and working up toward my lungs—and slowly exhale. This helps reduce my heart rate and my tension level. After making sure my arms and shoulders are relaxed, I start my swing.

PAR-5 STRATEGY: PLAYING BACKWARD

As an amateur, I used to walk each hole backward, from the green to the tee. By scoping out the hole that way, I got a better idea of where I wanted to hit every shot. On some par-5s, that meant laying up to a spot 80 or 100 yards out instead of going for the green in two. I'd rather

The biggest question to ask yourself on par-5 holes is, "Can I reach the green in two?" If not, there's no advantage to hitting driver off the tee. Opt for a fairway wood instead.

have a full wedge shot into a green than a tricky pitch or long bunker shot.

In my amateur days I couldn't reach many par-5s in two—maybe one out of every four. So it made sense to hit a fairway wood off the tee and then lay up to a full-wedge distance. Today, I'm driving the ball about 40 yards longer and can

reach most of the par-5s in two. If I hit my driver, a good tee shot can put me in excellent position to make birdie, maybe even eagle. Even if I hit my second shot into a greenside bunker, I'm still in great position to get on in three.

The biggest question to ask yourself on par-5 holes is, "Can I reach the green in two?" If not, there's no advantage to hitting driver off the tee. Opt for a fairway wood instead. You may even grip down an inch or two for extra control. The loft and shorter shaft of the club will help you hit the fairway. From there, the hole effectively becomes a short par-4; holing out in four will be well within your grasp.

From the fairway, lay up to a favorite distance (mine is 80 yards, a full lob wedge for me). Take one club more when hitting over hazards, and one club less when hitting short, to guard against a thin shot. Consider the hole location—you want to place your lay-up shot where it gives you the best angle to the green.

. . . .

On long par-5s, opt for a more-lofted fairway wood off the tee. It will help keep you in the fairway, making the hole effectively play like a short par-4. For your second shot (*right*), choose a club that will leave you with a full-wedge shot into the green.

APPROACH SHOTS: PICK THE RIGHT CLUB

Before every tournament, my caddie walks the course to get a feel for how it's playing. Are the greens soft or hard? Do they have much slope to them? Are there any particular shots I should be practicing for that week? Terry and I devise a strategy for how I'll attack, and soon we have a game plan in place. I know what kind of shots I want to play, where I want to land the ball, and where I don't want to hit it. During a round we consider all these factors plus the wind, the pin position (the course provides a daily pin sheet), the lie, the temperature, and how I'm swinging the club that day.

Terry gives me a yardage to the front of the green, as well as the yardage from there to the pin. Then we determine how far I want to carry the ball. That's the yardage I play to—not the total distance of the shot, but where I want to land the ball. He might say, "130 front, 17 pin," which means the pin is 147 yards (130 plus 17) away. If the green is flat and firm, I'll probably land the ball halfway (from the front edge) at 138 yards and let it release toward the hole. If the green is soft, I might carry the ball to the flag, knowing it won't roll much.

Occasionally I'll also ask Terry how many yards of green I have to the left and right of the pin. I'm not going to hit the ball perfectly straight every time, so it helps to have a little margin for error on both sides. For example, if there's 15 yards of green to the right of the flag, but only five yards to the left—where a deep, greenside bunker lurks—I'll "borrow" a few yards to the right of the hole and aim there.

Golf is not just a game of great shots. It's a game of bad shots, too. The champions are the ones who hit the fewest bad shots—and who are smart enough to keep their bad shots from being terrible.

· ·

My caddie, Terry McNamara, and I discuss club selection during my round of 59 in March 2001. When choosing a club, we determine where I want to land the ball (i.e., the carry distance). This is the yardage I play to, not the total distance to the flag.

LONG APPROACHES: AIM FOR THE MIDDLE

On Tour, we seldom see the pin in the middle of the green on a par-5, because they're not designed to handle a long approach. It is usually tucked behind a bunker or placed on a shelf. In these instances, I'll play for the middle of the green (*below*), using the most-lofted club I can. It's easier to land a high, soft 7-wood than a long iron that flies lower with less spin.

I use a similar strategy on long par-4s. If I have a 4- or 7-wood in my hands, I'm not going directly at the flag. I need some room for error because the longer the club, the bigger the space you need to land the ball. In many cases, I'll hit my approach short of the green and try to run it up. I'd rather be short and take my chances chipping than go over the green, where I might face a tricky recovery.

Always consider where you might end up if you hit a less than perfect shot. Again, when in doubt, play it safe. You'll save a couple of strokes per round.

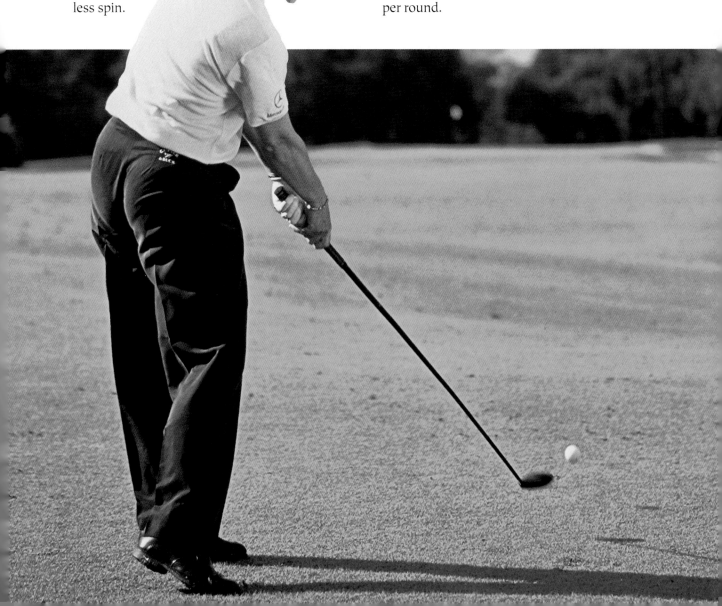

THERE'S NO 7½-IRON

When I'm between clubs (say choosing between a hard 8-iron or soft 7), my only thought is to land the ball on the green. If the pin is up front or there's trouble short of the green, I'll take the longer club and fly the ball past the pin. If the flagstick is on the back part of the green and there are hazards beyond, I'll take the shorter club and leave the ball short of the pin.

I also consider how my state of mind is. If I've been striking the ball well or my adrenaline is really pumping, I'll opt for the lesser of the two clubs.

PAR-3 STRATEGY: TAKE MORE CLUB

It's strange: Most of the amateurs I play with hit too much club on par-5s and not enough on par-3s. Ego plays a large factor on shorter holes—they think they hit the ball farther than they really do. Instead of playing to the average distance they hit each club, they play expecting a career shot every time.

Most par-3s are designed with hazards short of the green or on the sides. For that reason alone, you should think about hitting one more club. It's better to be a little long—and have a downhill putt or a short chip to the hole—than to be hitting from a greenside bunker or, worse, from the drop zone. By taking one extra club, you can also make less than perfect contact and still reach the green.

Be wary of "sucker pins" on these short holes. Three is a great score on a par-3, so don't get greedy: Aim for the fattest part of the green—you can two-putt for par while the suckers in your group make double bogeys.

ONCE BITTEN, TWICE SHY

I only like to take one risk per hole. If I'm aggressive off the tee and land the ball in the bushes, I'm going to play the next shot conservatively—punch it back into play. At least I'll be in the fairway. I won't play a risky shot over or through the trees, because compounding one mistake with another is how you make 6's and 7's and shoot a high number. On the other hand, if I crush my drive right down the middle, I may play the next shot aggressively, too.

My pro-am playing partners are always taking risks. A good example: One time, we were hitting our third shots from a bunker 50 yards short of the green—not an easy shot, by any means. On this particular par-5 hole, there was another bunker just short of the green, and the pin was tucked behind the bunker. Instead of playing it safe and firing at the center of the green, all of my partners went right at the flag. Several of the balls wound up plugging in the greenside bunker, making it near impossible to get up and down for par. They would have been much better off playing for the center of the green, two-putting, and walking away with a par.

More risks usually equals more strokes. This photo shows me after I've hit my tee shot into deep rough, just short of a fairway bunker. The ball is also above my feet, which means it will tend to curve left—toward the trees. I made my aggressive play off the tee; now it's time to be conservative. So rather than fire at the flag, I'm going to aim for the right edge of the green, away from the trouble. Even if I come up short, I'll have a chance to get up and down for par— a par I'll gladly take from this lie.

I like to take only one risk per hole. In the photo here, I've drawn a terrible lie in the rough, with the ball well above my feet. A jungle of trees and bushes lurks to my left, so rather than go directly at the flag—which is on the far left-hand side of the green— I'm going to aim at the right edge of the green, hitting away from the trouble.

MATCH PLAY: ONE AT A TIME

In stroke play, I try to mind my own business, play my own game, and put up a good score. In match play, I have to pay attention to what my opponent is doing. If she finds a fairway bunker off the tee, I might hit a shorter, more-lofted club, to make sure I'm short of the hazard—even if I have the length to clear it. I hold the advantage, so there's no sense in trying to blast it 30 yards past her ball.

But I'm careful not to play *too* conservatively. In match play, every hole is like a new match. If I birdie to go 1-up, I try to get to 2-up on the next hole, then 3-up, and so on. This is something I impressed upon Suzann Pettersen, an up-and-coming star on the LPGA Tour and my partner in two matches at the 2003 Solheim Cup in Sweden. "We don't want to settle for being 1-up," I told her. "We want to keep applying the pressure." It worked, as we won both our matches to help Europe to a 17-10 win over the Americans. And it was Suzann who sank the biggest putt of the biennial competition: a 15-foot birdie putt on the 18th hole in four-ball competition to give us a 1-up victory over Kelly Robbins and Laura Diaz. I got so emotional after that putt, I leaped into Suzann's arms.

Playing each hole as if it were a new match keeps your mind in the present. It's easy to think, "If I make this putt I'm 1-up, and then if I win the next hole I'm 2-up." Then suddenly your opponent chips in from off the green and you find yourself 1-down. That's deflating.

You can't assume anything. The only shots you have control over are your own, and you need to take them one at a time.

· ·

Here I am reacting to a birdie putt during morning foursomes at the 2003 Solheim Cup in Barseback, Sweden. In match play, I like to treat every hole like it's a new match. This way, my mind is constantly in the present, not in the past or future. The strategy has worked: My overall Solheim Cup match record is 16-8-3.

WALK THIS WAY

I've compiled a pretty good match play record over the years: 16-8-3 in six Solheim Cups (through 2003), including a 9-1-1 mark in four-somes (alternate shot) competition. Part of it is attitude. In match play it's important to suggest that you're in charge out there, no matter what the score is.

As Suzann and I prepared for our first match together in 2003, I gave her this advice: "Walk with your head up, like a champion. And walk fast. We want to be the first ones to

reach our tee shots, and the first ones on the green." Being first gives you the feeling that you're in the driver's seat out there. That instills confidence during a match, and sometimes leads your opponents to press when they really don't have to.

TAKING THE LOW ROAD

During the summer of 2000 I had a great run, winning four of six events in one stretch, including an unlikely one-shot victory over Rosie Jones at the JAL Big Apple Classic in New Rochelle, New York. It was unexpected because of the approach shot I hit on the 396-yard, par-4 17th hole at Wykagyl Country Club. I had birdied the par-5 15th to move into a tie with Rosie at 6-under, and after a par on 16, I pulled my tee shot on 17 into the left rough, 132 yards from the flag. I had a big tree in front of me and the fairways were very soft from days of rain. I had to hit something low but hard—hard enough to scoot all the way to the green. I decided on a three-quarter 7-iron, and lo and behold, the ball finished pin high, 15 feet from the hole! (Don't ask me to do it again.) I made the putt for birdie, then hung on for victory with a par on 18.

When hitting a low shot, your thinking should be counterintuitive: *Don't* hit down on the ball. The steeper the angle of approach, the more the ball will shoot up in the air. I start by playing the ball farther back in my stance, which delofts the clubface. I distribute a little more weight on my left side, and then make a three-quarter swing at three-quarter speed, finishing with my hands lower than normal—about chest high. A slower swing helps reduce the backspin on the ball and lowers its trajectory, and the low finish keeps my hands leading the club through impact, which keeps the ball low.

HOOKS AND SLICES

The first bogey I made at the Colonial was disheartening, especially after my recovery shot from off the fairway on the brutal, 470-yard, par-4 5th hole. Up to that point I had not missed a fairway the entire round, which for me began on the 10th hole. My tee shot at No. 5 took a bad hop and skipped left, leaving me with about 200 yards to the flag. Needing to curl the ball around a tree, I hit a roundhouse hook with my 4-iron, running the ball to the corner of the green some 60 feet from the hole. But I couldn't get it up and down from there—so much for my string of nine straight pars.

To make the ball hook, you need to play a more exaggerated version of the draw I covered in Chapter 3. I move the ball farther back in my stance, which promotes the inside path I need to hit the ball from right to left. I close my stance so my feet point to the right of the target, and aim the clubface at the target (*inset, right*). From there, I concentrate on swinging the club around my body, aggressively releasing the toe of the club past the heel (*right*). The ball should start to the right, where my body is pointing, and curve sharply left because the clubhead is closed at impact.

To make it slice, I play the ball forward and open my stance so that I'm pointing left of the target (*inset, left*); again aiming the clubface at

the target. The ball will start left, thanks to my out-to-in swing path, and curve back to the right because the clubface was open at impact (*left*). The more slice I need, the more I open my stance and abbreviate the finish.

To hit an intentional slice, move the ball forward in your stance, aim your body left of the target, and swing along your body line (*photos, left*). To hit a hook, move the ball back, aim right, and swing around your body, releasing the toe past the heel (*photos, above*).

ROUGH DECISION

When I teed off in the final round of the 1995 U.S. Women's Open, I trailed Meg Mallon by five strokes. I had nothing to lose, so I went after every shot and every putt aggressively, and played terrific golf over the first 14 holes. By the time I reached the par-4 11th hole at The Broadmoor, I had a one-shot lead over Meg. My drive on the 11th hole landed in the thick rough, but then I hit one of the best trouble shots of my career, wedging the ball seven feet from the hole. I made that putt for my third birdie in a row and a two-stroke lead—

just enough to stave off Meg.

Before I hit out of the rough, I evaluate the lie: *How much grass is covering the ball? Which way is the grass growing? How thick is it?* If the ball is nearly covered, I'll take a wedge and just pitch it back to the fairway. If the ball looks like it's teed up and might come out really hot—a flyer— I'll take less club than I would

normally hit from the same distance. (The more grass that comes between the ball and the clubface, the less backspin you can put on the ball—that's how you get a flyer.)

When hitting a full shot from the rough, my swing is more V-shaped—that is, steep—to minimize the amount of grass between the ball and clubface. I play the ball in the middle of my stance, setting about 60 percent of my weight on my left side (*far left*). I grip down on the club an inch and stand just a little closer to the ball than normal.

On the backswing, I hinge my wrists earlier than I normally would, which sets the club on a steeper

plane (*center*). The feeling is that my right arm never leaves my body in the backswing. On the downswing, I want calm acceleration as the clubhead cuts through the grass (*left*). Think *calm and smooth* as you hit this shot. The harder you swing, the more likely it is that you'll hit the shot fat, taking too much grass.

ANNIKA'S KEYS TO COURSE STRATEGY

My two biggest strengths on the golf course are my iron game and my mind. I'm like my own coach on the course, developing a strategy for attacking each hole and each shot. It's that kind of preparation that allows me to perform my very best when the pressure is on.

- On the tee, aim for the widest part of the fairway, taking one less club and playing short of hazards if necessary.
- Don't try a risky shot unless you can execute it at least six times out of ten.
- On approach shots, consider the firmness of the greens, the wind, and the pin positions, and choose a club according to where you want to land the ball, not just the distance to the flag.
- The longer the club, the more room you need to land the ball.
- Avoid big, ugly scores by taking a maximum of one risk per hole; don't compound one mistake by making another.

VISION54™

WHY NOT BIRDIE EVERY HOLE?

Every year I raise the bar on my performance. Why? Because it's important not to limit yourself. Before the 2003 season, my goal was to win more majors, and I won two—the McDonald's LPGA Championship and the Women's British Open. The year before, I set out to match Mickey Wright's LPGA record of 13 victories in a season. I won 11 on the LPGA Tour and 13 worldwide.

My ultimate goal? That's easy. It's to shoot 54—i.e., to birdie every hole on a par-72 course. It's been my vision since I joined the Swedish National Amateur Team in 1987. A few years later I met Pia Nilsson, my good friend, frequent sounding board, and positive-thinking guru. Pia, who coached the Swedish National Team from 1990 to '98, and mental consultant Kjell Enhager, author of the book *Quantum Golf*, believed that many players on the Swedish team held beliefs that limited them as golfers and people. To help them break down those barriers, they came up with the concept of VISION54™. The idea was based on the premise that if you play your home course enough times, you will eventually birdie every hole. So why not birdie them all in the same round?

It made sense to me. Why, for example, is it considered acceptable to two-putt every green? If you think that's okay, you'll expect to take two putts. But if you believe it's possible to one-putt each green, you can.

VISION54 is always in the back of my mind. In fact, in my golf bag, I have a knitted head cover with the number 54 on it. It's not so much the number that counts, it's the idea that you can birdie every hole. In 2001, I rallied from 10 strokes back in the final round to win The Office Depot Tournament in Los Angeles. All day I kept telling myself, *Hey, you need to birdie in*. That's the vision that inspires me to push the boundaries of what is possible.

59 REASONS TO BELIEVE

The morning I shot 59, I warmed up for an hour and 15 minutes, just as I do before every round—putting, chipping, and hitting balls on the range. There was nothing unusual about how I felt or hit the ball. I just wanted to take advantage of my early morning tee time, because of the softer conditions. So I was aggressive from the start, and the round built from there.

I teed off on the par-5 10th hole—at 534 yards, the longest at Moon Valley Country Club—and I immediately struck for birdie after hitting a sand wedge nine feet from the pin. Next came birdies at 11 and 12, including a curling 30-foot putt up and over a ridge on No. 12. That was the first sign it might be my day. After I birdied 13, I asked my caddie, Terry, "How many birdies is that?"

He said it was four.

"Well, I've done six in a row before," I said. "Let's keep it going." Next thing I knew, I was at 6-under, then 7, then 8.

After a par on the 9th hole—and the string of birdies finally broken—I proceeded to birdie the next four holes, with the help of a miraculous 22-foot putt on No. 2. It was a very tricky line and the putt went uphill and then down—the most difficult putt to gauge in terms of speed. When that one went in, I told my sister Charlotta, whom I happened to be paired with that day, that I was going to buy a lottery ticket as soon as the round ended. Everything was falling in place.

A birdie on No. 4 moved me to 12-under par—12 birdies in 13 holes—and suddenly I was one stroke away from 59. I remember shooting a glance at the leaderboard and seeing all these red numbers up there. What a sight!

As much as my mind was wandering between shots, I was still focused when I stood over the ball. I kept reminding myself, *The ball doesn't know how many under par you are or how many under you can be. Just hit it from here to there.* After three pars and a birdie to move to 13-under, I had a chance to shoot 58 with a final birdie on the 9th hole, a tight par-4 with water on the left and bunkers on the right. After a perfect drive down the middle, I had 112 yards to the pin. That's normally an easy approach, but not at Moon Valley, and not that day. Any shot that went long and left of the flag would feed sharply toward the 10th tee, making it next to impossible to get up and down for par.

Terry wanted me to play it safe and aim to the right, but I told him, "No, I'm going right at the flag. I want to shoot 58."

My sand wedge approach came down about 12 inches to the right of the hole and stopped 10 feet away. I then grazed the left edge with my birdie effort and tapped in for my 59. Once the ball fell, I started to count quickly to myself, to make sure I had shot 59, not 60. I looked at Terry and said, "I did shoot 59, didn't I?"

He said, "Yeah, you did."

And then I jumped into his arms.

· ·

Once I realized that I had indeed shot 59, becoming the first LPGA player ever to break 60, I leapt into my caddie's arms. On that magical day in March 2001, I birdied 12 of my first 13 holes. I needed only 25 putts, hit all 18 greens in regulation and 13 of 14 fairways. I never saw a bunker.

FACE THE FEAR

What did I learn that day? For starters, I decided I would never wish for a par again. After eight holes, the thought of being 8-under par was a major burden to carry. As I stood on the 18th tee—the ninth hole I played—I actually told Terry, "I have to make a par here." After leaving a birdie putt three feet short, I knew I had given in to my fear.

The next time I make eight birdies in a row, I'll try as hard as I can to make it nine in

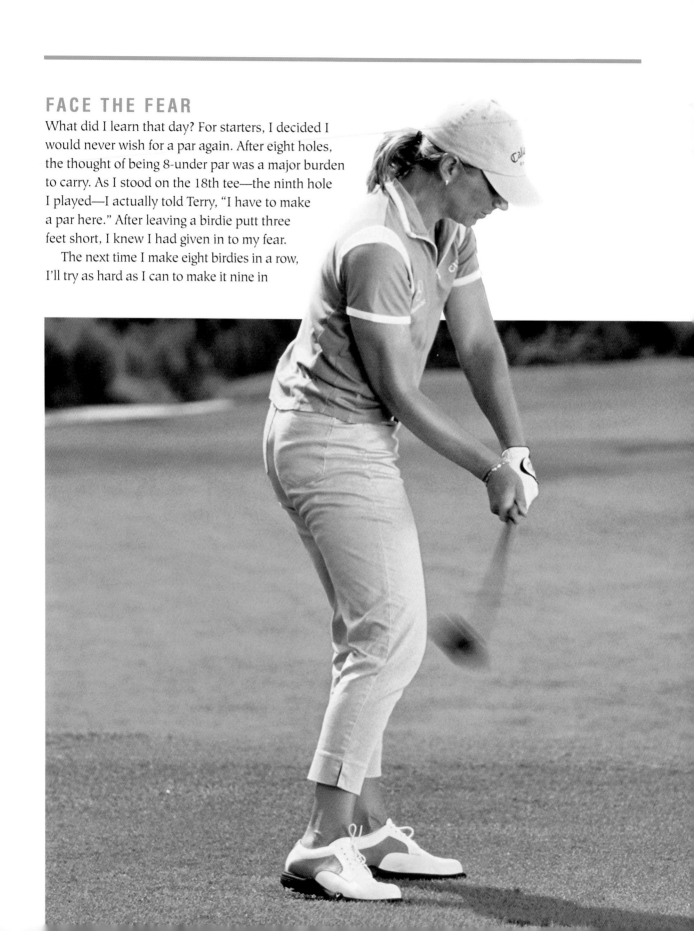

a row. I won't be afraid of shooting a low score again because I've done it now. I've faced my fear.

"Face the Fear" is an expression I first heard from Kjell Enhager, who in addition to being a golf pro is a ski instructor. When I was a freshman at the University of Arizona in 1990, I was having a hard time dealing with the sharp desert shadows of Tucson afternoons. I'd see my shadow moving with my swing and it was hard to maintain focus. I talked with Kjell about it, and he told me a story about a skiing accident he once had in Austria. Kjell was tumbling out of control down a steep slope, and instead of leaning away from the hill, toward the danger below, he was leaning back into the slope. But that only made the fall worse. So he faced his fear and began to lean forward, killing his fall and probably saving his life.

That shadow was my nemesis, and instead of turning my back to it I had to learn to deal with it. It was similar to the nervousness I felt making speeches back in my junior playing days. I would three-putt the final hole of a tournament on purpose, just to avoid giving a victory speech. Obviously, I overcame that fear, and the more speeches I gave, the more comfortable I became in front of a microphone.

I remember the first time I shot under par on my par-73 home course, Bro-Balsta, just north of Stockholm. I was 17 and as I walked down the 15th fairway, I couldn't help but obsess about what I needed to do on the last few holes to shoot 72. *Okay*, I told myself, *I can't afford a bogey.* I had been close many times, but on that day I managed to break through in a big way—I shot 69! Afterward, I thought, *What's the big deal?*

The key to achieving excellence is to be unafraid of it. If you dare to be the best, you need to have the courage to do whatever is necessary to see your vision through, even if it means doing things differently than others.

While I attended the University of Arizona, I had to overcome the distraction of seeing my shadow move (*left*) when I played. I eventually learned to deal with it and "face my fear."

A little reminder to myself to not be afraid of the consequences.

NO MORE FEAR

Before the final round of the 2001 Nabisco Championship, I wrote a note on my visor in Swedish. Loosely translated, it said, "Don't Be Afraid. Face the Fear." It had been five years since I won a major championship, and I couldn't let this chance slip away. On each hole, I told myself, "You're right where you want to be. You've been in this position before and won, now do it again."

Normally, I look at the leaderboard three or four times a hole, but that day, I barely glanced at it. Instead, I stared at my visor and drew inspiration from those words. I started the day a stroke back of Rachel Teske, but after birdies on 4, 7, and 11, I had a two-shot lead. After giving a stroke back with a bogey on 12, I birdied 13 to regain my two-shot advantage. Down the stretch, I stayed calm. I capped my round of three-under-par 69 with a 25-footer for birdie on No. 18—and a most refreshing swim in Champions Lake.

GET "IN THE ZONE"

What was unusual about my 59 at Moon Valley was that I never thought about a second putt on any hole. Some days I'm so focused on the second putt that I don't hit the first one hard enough. But that day, I kept thinking, *There's the hole, it breaks a cup to the left, hit it there.* I wasn't thinking about the consequences if I missed. It was like that on my full swings, too. On the final hole, I wasn't concerned about losing it left and shooting 60. I went after that shot, trying to shoot 58.

Everything felt so easy that day. That's how it is when you're "in the zone." You look at a putt

The more time you spend thinking about the negative consequences of your actions, the more likely you are to make those thoughts real.

and read it perfectly. You choose a club and you know it's the right yardage. You could swing with your eyes closed and the ball would go dead straight. The fairways look like runways, and the holes are as big as manhole covers.

If there's a lesson to be learned from being in this elusive zone, it's simply this: Don't fear any consequences. Sure, you want to play smart, but you can't play afraid. I see a lot of my pro-am playing partners glance at the target, then fix their eyes on the sand traps, water, hazards, and other trouble areas. That only sends stress signals to the brain.

The more time you spend thinking about the negative consequences of your actions, the more likely you are to make those thoughts real. If your last thought before taking the club back is, *Don't hit it in the water*, then your brain will focus on the water, not your target. Instead of stressing about the water, try carrying a single positive thought or image into your swing, such as, *follow through to a complete finish*. You'll be surprised how easy it is to be brave.

STAY IN THE MOMENT

Many thoughts race through my head during a round. I may picture myself winning the tournament or shooting 54. But once I'm about to hit a shot, that's all I'm thinking about. I'm focused on the moment. I try never to let the outcome of the last shot or the potential of the next one affect that focus.

I learned to treat each shot as if it were the most important one of the round when I was with the Swedish National Team. Pia often had us play six individual three-hole matches during the course of a round. The goal was to win each match. If, for example, you had an 18 handicap, you got a stroke per hole against par. If you played three holes in 3 over par, you tied that match. Score bogey-bogey-par (2 over) and you won.

Pia was trying to keep us focused on every hole, so we didn't start thinking ahead or back. And it worked.

TAKE A VACATION BETWEEN SHOTS

To score low, you must conserve your energy and focus for all 18 holes. One way to stay sharp is to "go on vacation" between shots. As you walk to your ball, talk to one of your playing partners about a movie or a ball game, or hum a tune to yourself. The idea is to take a time-out from golf, so you don't wear yourself down mentally.

Once you approach your ball, take 30 or 40 seconds to refocus. It might help to have a trigger point—something that gets your mind focused on golf again. For me, this point occurs when I'm standing behind my ball and my caddie sets my golf bag on the ground. That's when I click into focus and start my preshot routine (*right*).

The morning I shot 59, I really pushed myself. It was hard to think about anything but making birdie, but I tried. I was planning to cook a fish soup for Charlotta that night at her home in Phoenix, so I was thinking about what ingredients I would need. I was also thinking about how I would refurnish a room back at our house in Florida. As long as it wasn't golf, the thought refreshed me. Try it—it might help your cooking and home decor as well as your golf.

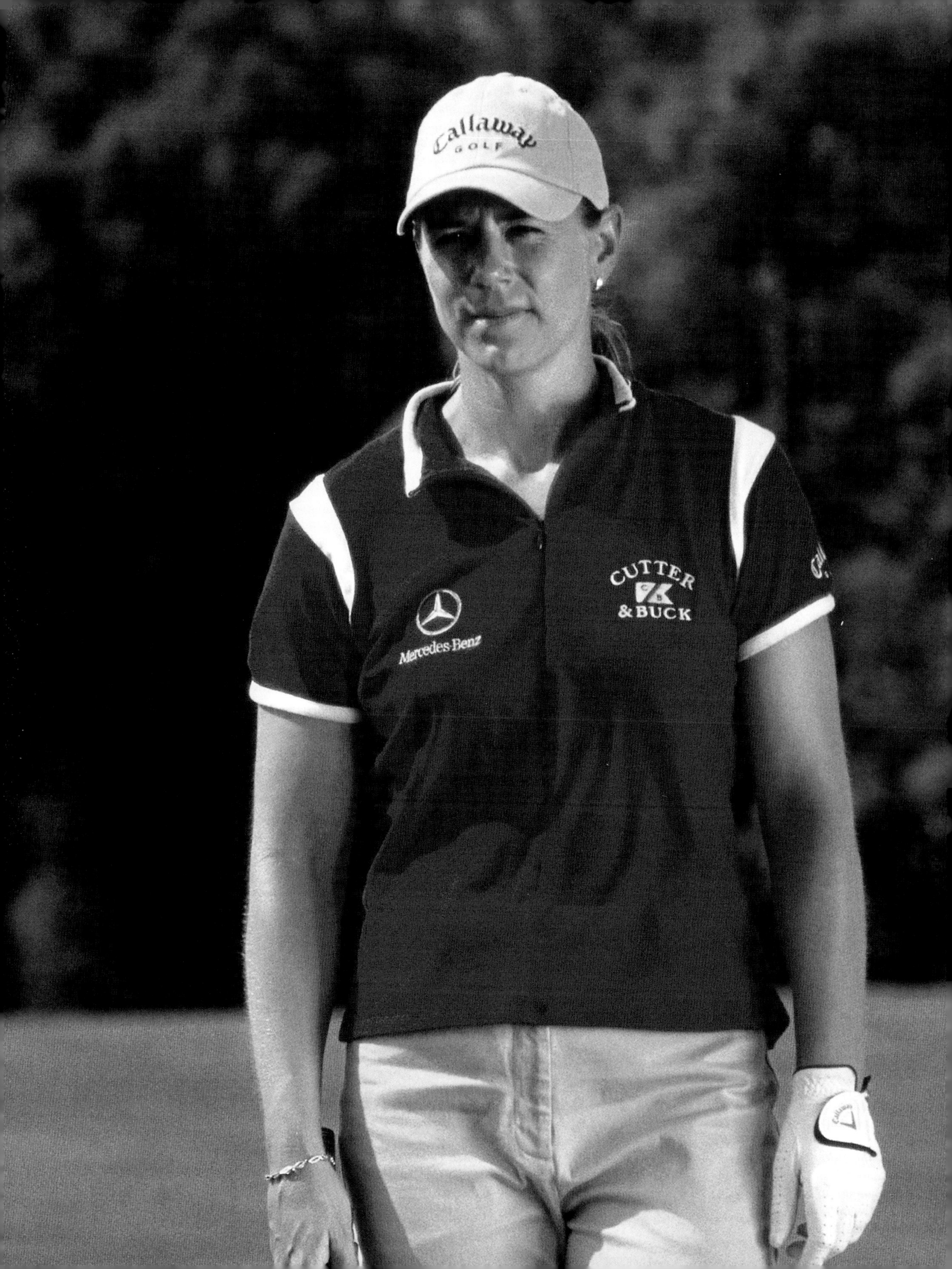
Callaway
GOLF
CUTTER
&BUCK
Mercedes-Benz

NO GEAR BELOW NEUTRAL

Early in my career, I carried a memo pad in my back pocket. I'd record my moods during the course of play—happy, aggressive, patient, focused. If my moods were darker—angry, frustrated, anxious—I'd refer to the notebook and try to recapture moments when my emotional state was better.

To achieve optimum performance, you must keep your emotions in check. You need to brush aside all feelings of anger, frustration, and doubt that can lead to poor performance. Pia used to tell her young golfers that we had two choices when it came to reacting to a shot: We could be happy, or we could be neutral. If we bombed a tee shot down the middle, we could pump our fists or jump for joy. But if we sliced a tee shot into the rough, we couldn't react negatively. Instead, we were to take a few seconds to replay the shot with the desired outcome in mind.

The idea was to avoid negative feelings, keeping everything no worse than neutral.

TAKE YOUR TIME WARMING UP

I try to maintain a consistent environment. That means surrounding myself with a solid support team, getting a good night's sleep, eating well, and arriving at the course in time to get a full warm-up. I don't like to feel rushed or stressed before I play.

The purpose of warming up is to get physically and mentally ready to play. I follow a strict routine that begins about an hour and 15 minutes before I tee off. After some putting and chipping, I head for the range. And then it's back to the practice green again to hit a few putts.

On the range, I start with my 60-degree wedge, then slowly work up to my 4-wood, hitting either the even- or odd-numbered clubs. Then it's back to my lob wedge before I start hitting driver. Tempo is crucial: I need to feel that I've found a good rhythm to my swing before I head out to the course.

On the putting green,

I follow the same build-up formula: I start with three-footers—using my right hand only—and then shift to two hands, gradually increasing distance as I get a feel for the speed of the greens that day. The reason I start with short putts is because I want to build some confidence for the round. If I miss the vast majority of my putts in practice, how can I expect to make many out on the course?

If I'm not swinging the club very well during warm-up, I'll deal with it after the round. I don't like to make swing changes during a tournament round. If I'm consistently hitting a fade on the range, I'll play for a fade that day.

My pre-round routine lasts a full hour and 15 minutes, and consists of putting, chipping (*opposite page*), and hitting balls. If I consistently hit the ball from left to right on the range, I'll play for a fade that day (*below*).

NUMBERS CRUNCHER

Pia once told me, "As soon as you think you have all the answers, you'll get beat by someone who is still learning." In other words, a golfer—or any athlete—must constantly look for ways to improve, gathering new knowledge, learning new shots, and setting loftier goals.

My quest for knowledge and inspiration can be found on my laptop computer. I've been keeping detailed statistics about my game as far back as college, creating spreadsheets to analyze such data as the number of fairways I've hit and missed (and whether I missed left or right), my percentage of up-and-downs from off the green, greens in regulation, putts made between six and fifteen feet (my birdie range), and so on. I track all of this information on the daily pin sheet that we pros get every day of a tournament, using a pencil to jot down such things as where I hit the fairway, how many yards I had for my approach, where I hit the green (if I hit it), and whether I took one, two, or three putts. I keep track of the length of each putt, and where it finished. Every couple of weeks, I gather all my worksheets and input the data into my computer. Then I study my strengths and weaknesses, and formulate a plan to attack the weaknesses.

When I first started crunching these numbers, my goal was to hit more fairways and greens. I discovered that I wasn't hitting greens because I wasn't driving the ball in the fairway. Today, I'm much more accurate—I'm now consistently among the leaders in both categories on the LPGA Tour.

In recent years, my attention has shifted to the short game. In 2000, I averaged a career-worst 30.41 putts per round. My stats showed that I wasn't making many putts from 12 feet and in, so I made this my mission in 2001, increasing the time I spent on the practice green by an hour a day. By the end of 2003, I had shaved nearly a full stroke (29.55) off my average. In the highly competitive world of pro golf, that's huge. But I'm not satisfied. My new goal for 2004 is to boost my percentage of up-and-downs inside 100 yards (both pitching and chipping) to 50 percent. In '03, my percentage was 33 percent.

Before you stow your clubs in the closet each winter, I would suggest you take inventory of your game. Use your last five rounds of the year to note where you're hitting, or missing, fairways; whether you tend to miss left or right; how often you get up and down around the green; and so on. You'll get an early jump on next season.

ANNIKA'S KEYS TO VISION54™

If you played your home course every day, you would eventually birdie every hole. So why not birdie them all in one round? It's not impossible.

- Don't turn your back on your fears; face them down.
- Stay in the moment. Limit your focus to one shot at a time rather than thinking about the last shot or the next one.
- "Go on vacation" between shots, then refocus on golf once you reach your ball.
- Make your last thought before taking the club back a positive one—something that will help you excel.
- Give yourself time to warm up—physically *and* mentally—before you play.

Staying

in Shape

···

GETTING FIT

Getting Fit

WORKOUT TIPS TO HELP YOUR GAME

I've worked hard to craft a swing that's simple and repeatable, but my workouts have also contributed to my success. My newfound strength gave me the endurance to win eight LPGA titles in 2001, eleven in 2002, and six more in 2003. My strength gave me the power to drive the ball more than 270 yards and the confidence to compete against the world's best male players at the 2003 Colonial.

For most of my career, I approached fitness the same way I did when I was a college student at Arizona. I hit the gym a few times a week, lifted some weights, and occasionally ran or swam. In the fall of 2001 I started working with Kai Fusser, a trainer in Orlando who's best known for his work with athletes from my second-favorite hobby after cooking, wakeboarding. Kai told me I'd been babying myself. He threw some tough exercises at me—pull-ups and squats with weights. Mastering these exercises gave me real confidence, which helped my game as much as my new strength.

The results have been amazing. I now hit three of every four par-5s in two; 10 years ago, I hit one of four. I ranked in the LPGA's top five in driving distance for the first time in 2002, and then led the category in 2003. And I got longer without losing my trademark accuracy, because the program Kai and I created not only made my golf muscles stronger, but also improved my balance, flexibility, and rotational power.

Now I'll show you the keys to my workouts. Whether you do these three to five days a week in the gym, as I do, or incorporate some of them into your own workouts, they're sure to help your game.

(Please note: I've given the amount of weight that I use for each exercise, but it's best to work with a trainer to determine the correct weight for you.)

A great swing starts with a balanced, athletic posture—the same posture you should use in the gym. First, make sure your feet are planted solidly on the ground. Your shoulders should be over your hips and ankles. Your spine should be straight. Most important, your abdominal muscles should be held in tightly. This posture will optimize your workouts and protect your back.

· · · · · · · · · ·

Good posture in the gym carries over to the golf course.

STRONG TO THE CORE

Your core—the muscles of your back and mid-section—provides power and keeps you stable during the swing. These exercises will increase your rotational power and make your core muscles stronger.

SUPERWOMAN

This exercise, which works the entire body while targeting the lower back, can be done two ways. The first is easy: Lie over a physio ball with your body stretched out. With your abs pulled in tight, lift your left hand off the floor. Do the same with your right leg. Hold for a second, lower, and then repeat eight to ten times. Switch sides.

Once your strength improves, try this the tough way: with your knees on the ball.

Working with a personal trainer can really keep you motivated. You'll never get bored with your workouts, and it's great to have someone push you harder than you would push yourself. To find someone qualified, look for a trainer with a degree in physical therapy or exercise physiology and certification from the American College of Sports Medicine, the National Strength and Conditioning Association, or the American Council on Exercise.

MED-BALL TWIST

Here's a power-building exercise that's also a good pre-round warm-up. Stand in front of a mirror holding a four- to eight-pound medicine ball. Make sure your spine stays straight. Keeping your feet planted, rotate backward, and then change direction quickly to bring the ball forward again. Make sure your abdominals are in and tight the entire time, controlling the motion. Do three sets of eight to ten reps. Then switch sides. Start this exercise slowly and then quicken your rotation as you get stronger.

If you're working with a partner or trainer, toss the ball back and forth (*opposite page*). Try to use the power from your abs, not your arms, to catch and throw.

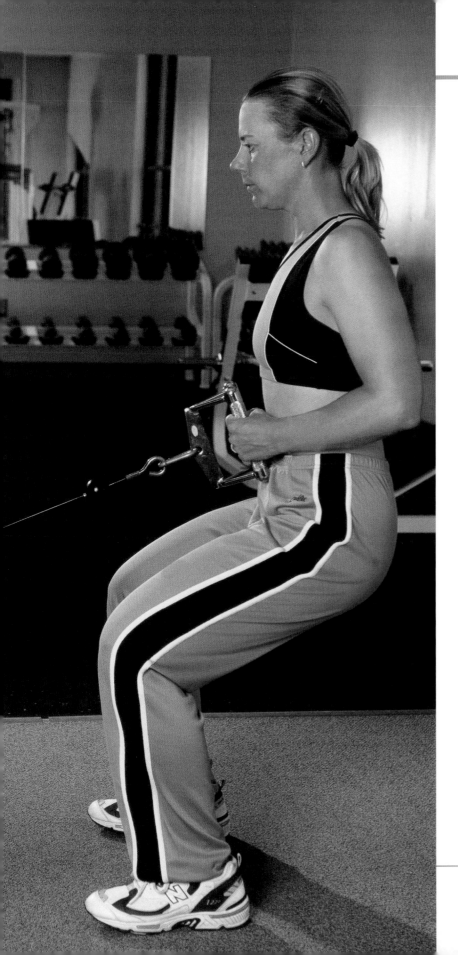

JOCKEY ROWS

This exercise works your entire body, but targets the abdominals. Set the weight on a cable-cross machine between 60 and 80 pounds and use a triangle bar as a handle. Keeping your abs in and tight the entire time, pull the bar away from the machine and get into a jockey position. Plant your feet firmly. Let the weight pull your upper body forward so that you feel a stretch along your back.

Now pull the bar to your belly button while your upper body rises to an upright position with your chest out and your shoulder blades back. Let the handle return to its start position. Do three sets of eight to ten reps.

· · · · · · · · · · · · · · · · ·

At the end of your sets, your muscles should feel exhausted, as if you could perform the exercise only one or two more times.

WOOD-CHOP UP

"Wood-chop up" targets the inner abdominals, which generate rotational power. Using a rope handle and 30 to 40 pounds on a cable-cross machine, start with your hands low to one side, your knees bent, and your spine straight. Pull the handle swiftly up and diagonally across your body. Hold briefly and then lower slowly with your arms extended. Feel your abs control the movement all the way down. Do three sets of eight to ten reps. Then switch sides.

WOOD-CHOP DOWN

This exercise also targets the inner abs, but now you rotate more around your spine, as in the golf swing. With the weight on a cable-cross machine between 30 and 60 pounds, start with your spine straight. Reach to the side to grab the rope handle. Rotate diagonally, from the top on one side to the bottom on the other. Keep rotating as long as you can keep your abs tight. Return slowly, keeping the arms fully extended. Do three sets of eight reps. Then switch sides.

NOW PUSH YOURSELF!

Here are a few toughies Kai sneaked into my workouts—exercises that pushed me a little harder and helped me gain twenty yards off the tee.

SQUATS

It took me a year to work up to squatting 300 pounds, and I began slowly. The best way to begin is without weights. Place a bench behind you and move down as if you're going to sit on the bench. Make sure your hips move first, not your knees. Engage your abdominals on the way down and up. When you can easily do eight of these, add light dumbbells on your shoulders. Then, when you can comfortably squat with twenty pounds on each shoulder, switch to a barbell.

PULL-UPS

Most women—and many men—can't do pull-ups. It took a month of trying before I could do two, and another year for me to get up to fourteen, so don't be discouraged if it takes you a while.

Beginners should start in the bent-arm finish position, either raised by a partner or while stepping up from a bench. Now lower yourself. Once you can control this move, start pulling yourself up. When you can easily do ten, add a bit of weight on a weight belt.

• • • • • • • •
**Use a mirror
to check your
form.**

TWISTING BICEP CURLS

Bicep curls are a weight-lifting staple, but mine
have a twist. Start with the palms turned in so
that you work your wrists and forearms—muscles
that are vital to the short game. Hold a pair of
eight- to twenty-five-pound dumbbells with your
palms turned toward your body. Bring your forearms up, twisting your palms toward your body
on the way. Do three sets of eight to ten reps.

SHOULDER CABLE CROSS

Set eight to twenty pounds on a cable-cross machine and grab the handle with one hand. Pull the handle up diagonally across your body. Make sure your spine stays straight. Hold briefly, return slowly. Do three sets of eight reps, then switch sides.

love to cook and to eat, so it's tough for me to follow a rigid diet. But as an athlete, I am careful about what I put into my body, especially on game days. Here are some of my tips for eating right and keeping up your energy during a round.

- Try to eliminate highly processed foods, like white flour and simple sugars, from your diet. They can cause your energy to spike and dip.
- Eat as many organic raw fruits and vegetables as you can to get needed vitamins and enzymes.
- Try to maintain a caloric balance of about 20 percent protein, 60 percent complex carbohydrates, and 20 percent fat in your meals.
- The most important meal to get right is breakfast; it sets the tone for the rest of the day. My favorite choices are whole-grain cereal with soy-milk, or a couple of eggs with whole-grain toast, and fresh fruit.

MIX IT UP TO GET AS STRONG AS YOU CAN

There's no such thing as a typical Annika work-out. My workouts are like my rounds—each is different, with new challenges and lessons. Along with my trainer, Kai Fusser, I devised a plan that builds me into peak condition in the off-season and helps me stay strong and flexible all year. The program is complicated, but you can benefit from some of the essentials:

My plan starts with general strengthening exercises, moves to heavy weights, and ends with a combination of strength and speed training. By the end my golf muscles are firing smoothly at optimum speed. You can work with a trainer to make the same sort of progress.

- The body adapts quickly, so vary your exercises day to day. Variety keeps your muscles, nervous

- Snack halfway through your round to keep your energy level up, but avoid greasy hamburgers and hot dogs. Some of my favorite snacks are bananas, Kraft Balance Bars (1:3), sandwiches of almond butter and honey or jelly on whole-wheat bread, and protein or meal-replacement shakes (they're easy to use and to digest).
- Drink at least eight ounces of water before your round, and keep drinking water during it. On a hot day, I can go through a bottle of water every one or two holes.
- I live by the 80-20 rule: I'm vigilant 80 percent of the time, but I like to enjoy an occasional dessert, glass of wine, or bowl of white pasta. It's easier to stick to a healthful diet if you know you can occasionally break the rules.

MY FAVORITE MEAL

Here's a dish that I love to cook when I'm on the road—or just relaxing at home:

Annika's Thai Chicken Pasta: (4 servings)

1 lb chicken breast	Marinade:	1 tsp soy sauce
2 cups half-and-half	2 tbsp olive oil	2 pressed garlic cloves
1 lb fresh penne pasta	4 tbsp chili sauce (I use Heinz)	2 tsp ground ginger

Cut the chicken into small pieces. Mix the marinade and add the chicken. Let it sit for two hours. Heat up a pan and add the chicken and marinade. Add the half-and-half and cook until the chicken is done. Add additional garlic, chili, and ginger to taste. Serve with fresh-cooked penne pasta.

system, and mind stimulated. Again, working with a trainer is a good way to keep it fresh.
- After you work one muscle group—arms, legs, etc.—give that area a week to recuperate. It takes two days for muscles to rebuild themselves, and another three to four days for them to regain their previous strength.
- The next time you work that muscle group, increase the resistance a little.
- When weightlifting, your muscles should feel exhausted—as if you couldn't continue—at the end of eight to ten reps.
- Don't exercise for more than an hour. You'll lose concentration and overload your nervous system. Working out longer than you should can also hurt your concentration.

NO SLIPS, NO ERRORS

Good balance gives your swing a strong, solid base. I spend five to ten minutes per workout on balance—that's the right amount of time to teach your nervous system something new. Physio balls and balance pads can help. You can stand on balance pads or cushions while you lift free weights, or even when you swing a golf club. Here are two exercises guaranteed to improve your balance.

GET ON BOARD

Balance boards are fun and easy. Start by holding on to something with the board resting on grass, then move to carpeting, and finally to a hard floor. When you can control yourself without swaying, try swinging a golf club.

ON THE BALL

Here's an advanced exercise—standing on a physio ball while swinging a weighted bar. I didn't just jump up there one day; I worked up to it. I started by trying to kneel on the ball, and then to kneel and swing, and then to stand on the ball. You'll need something stable to hold on to (I used the cable-cross machine) until your balance improves.

Good balance is a must when you're playing on windy days, or hitting from uneven lies and bunkers. If your body is stable, it'll be easier to get the clubface in the right position on these types of shots.

STRETCH YOUR LIMITS

Many of my exercises are performed using my full range of motion, so they stretch and strengthen at the same time. I spend extra time stretching crucial areas that tend to tighten up. Always warm up with five to ten minutes of cardio before you stretch—otherwise the stretching has no lasting effect.

SHOULDER STRETCHES

With your feet shoulder-width apart and your palms down, grasp a bar with both hands and bend at the knees. Let your weight stretch your arms, shoulders, and back. Hold for 45 seconds to a minute, then repeat with your palms up.

Next, turn away from the bar and, with your feet planted shoulder width apart, grasp with your palms down. Lean forward until you feel a stretch in your arms, chest, and shoulders. Hold for 45 seconds to a minute, then repeat with palms up.

• • • • • • • • • • • • • • •

Many people stretch before they exercise, but it's more effective to stretch at the end of your workouts, when your muscles are loose and warm.

HAMSTRING STRETCHES

Tight hamstrings can cause an imbalance that strains your lower back, so I try to do these every day. Kai is helping me here, but you can also grab your calf with your hands or put a towel around your foot. Slowly pull your leg toward your upper body. Hold for 45 seconds to a minute. If your leg starts to shiver or shake, release for a couple of seconds and then resume the stretch. Switch legs.

GOAL PATROL

I go to the gym five days a week when I'm not playing, three days a week when I am. You may think I'm a super-motivated machine, but trust me—there are days when I'd rather sit on the couch and watch The Food Network than sweat through a workout. But getting stronger has helped me reach my goals, and my goals keep me motivated to do things I don't always feel like doing. You can do the same—and it's not as hard as you might think.

First, ask yourself why you want to get stronger. Is it to add yards to your drives? To keep up your stamina at the end of a round? Or just to look and feel better? Decide what you want to accomplish, write it down, and then monitor your progress. Focusing on your goals will help you reach them.

HEART SMART

Being strong and fit has helped my focus and concentration. I used to feel tired at the end of a round of golf—and especially after four days of tournament golf—but now I have tons of energy.

This counters what many golfers believe, but your cardiovascular health affects your game. The fitter your heart, the more endurance you'll have and the faster your body will recover

The only way to know whether you are performing high- or low-intensity cardiovascular exercise is by monitoring your heart rate. Take your age and subtract it from 220. That's your maximum heart rate. When your heart rate reaches 60 to 65 percent of the maximum, you are performing low-intensity exercise. When it reaches 80 to 90 percent of the max, you are performing high-intensity exercise. Example for a 35-year-old:

- 220
- -35
- 185 beats/minute = maximum heart rate
- 185 x .60 = 111 beats/minute (low intensity)
- 185 x .90 = 167 beats/minute (high intensity)

from exertion. Also, your heart will be less likely to pound in pressure situations. And the last thing you want standing over a crucial putt is for your heart to race because you just climbed a hill.

The best way to train your heart to recover quickly from exertion is to mix low-intensity cardiovascular exercise with regular spurts of high intensity. (See the heart-rate sidebar to determine high and low intensity.) Whether you ride a stationary bike, jog, or use a Stairmaster (I love to run, swim, mountain bike, and Rollerblade), intersperse every four to five minutes of low-intensity exercise with 30 seconds to a minute of high intensity. And, unless you're trying to lose weight, you don't need to do more than 20 to 25 minutes of cardio, two to three times a week.

SOREN-SLAM:
*Here I am posing with the trophy
following my victory in the 2003
Weetabix Women's British Open at
Royal Lytham & St. Annes Golf Club.
With the win, I became the sixth woman
to complete the career grand slam. My
other major triumphs were the 1995
and 1996 U.S. Women's Opens; the
2001 and 2002 Nabisco Championships;
and the 2003 McDonald's LPGA
Championships (inset).*